I0772602

AHEAD *of the* HOUNDS

RABBIT HOUSE PRESS
Versailles, KY 40383

First edition published by Crispin Press in 1988. Second edition published in 2024 by Rabbit House Press.

Published in the United States of America by Rabbit House Press, March 2024.

For inquiries about author appearances and/or volume orders contact us at rabbithousepress.com.

ISBN: 979-8-9871928-9-4

Editor: Erin Chandler
Cover art: Toss Chandler
Interior/Cover design & formatting; copy editor: Brooke Lee

AHEAD *of the* HOUNDS

Jonelle Fisher

RABBIT
HOUSE
PRESS
rabbithousepress.com

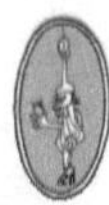

For their constant love and encouragement, this book is dedicated to my mother, Mary Clift Jones, and to the memory of my Father, John Robert Jones. It was he who taught me years ago that happiness in life is a matter of staying ahead of the hounds.

PART ONE

The Beginning

O, wind, O mighty melancholy wind
Blow through me, blow!
Thou blowest forgotten things into my mind
From long ago

—John Todhunter

1959

I want to practice medicine with Ben Roach.

—Jack

The letter was written from the office of Ben Roach, M.D., Midway, Kentucky on April 26th, 1959.

Dear Jack,

Ruth and I enjoyed very much seeing you last Thursday. Tonight, I want to write you to repeat in writing some of the things we talked about. My practice has grown so much that it is more than I can handle alone, especially so in the past year. In many ways, a two man practice seems to be better than solo work, and I believe would work unusually well here. Although our acquaintance is short, Ralph Denham had talked to me about you last December and his recommendation of you carries a great deal of weight with me. Ruth and I both liked you personally and feel that your friendly manner is excellent for this kind of practice.

We are very anxious for you to come to Midway because we are very fond of this town and its location and think it offers many advantages. You can drive here in less than two hours and could easily make it here and back to Louisville the same afternoon or evening. You may come anytime, and I expect your wife would be coming also to see for herself. Please talk with her and come on down any day, afternoon, or night. Just let us know before you come.

I know you are interested in the financial part also... I am willing to give you $10,000.00 for the first year, and to work out a full partnership after the first year if agreeable to us both. There are a number of 'fringe benefits' in addition to the salary that we could show you when you come to see us.

Jack, give us some consideration and write, phone, or come to see us.

Sincerely,
Ben

Shortly after my husband received this letter when he was interning at the Louisville General Hospital, we drove up to Midway to meet with Ben and Ruth to check things out. We walked all over the small town with them, met two of Ben's great-aunts, went to see the office and the hospital, had supper with them and were about to start home when a patient came knocking at the door with a small child in her arms who was crying with a sore throat. Ben took them into the living room and treated the child on the couch. He was tender and compassionate, yet totally professional. We were both impressed. It came as no surprise to me when, on the drive back to Louisville, Jack turned and said, "I want to practice medicine with Ben Roach."

We came to Midway one month later with two-year-old Jenny, Baby Matt, and thirty-three dollars to our name. Jack hit the ground running. They saw around seventy-five patients a day and were making house calls every night until the wee hours. They charged three dollars per office visit, five dollars per home visit, five dollars per hospital visit, seventy-five dollars to deliver a baby, and one dollar for a shot. Bills were sent whenever time allowed and sometimes payment came in the form of fresh vegetables, fruit, or meat and chickens. Sometimes it never came at all. No one was ever refused treatment for any reason whatsoever.

Medicine was so simple then, without Medicare or Medicaid, and without all the regulations and insurance forms. It was one on one, the patient and the doctor working together to combat disease and pain, and the patient paid if he could for services rendered directly to the doctor. When a patient came to the office in 1959, he usually had to wait a while before it was his turn to be seen, as they worked without appointments. Music would be playing, not piped in, not a fancy FM station, but records of old Broadway hits such as "L'il Abner" or "South Pacific." Sometimes they would repeat many times before one of the girls who worked there would have a minute to turn it over and play the other side.

Upon being taken back to one of the examining rooms, the patient would most likely have to wait a little longer. The rooms were small with window air-conditioning units, an examining table, a sink, and very little else. The urine specimen would be spun down in a hand cranked centrifuge in preparation for the microscope. X-Rays were taken in the middle room on a huge table that doubled as a lunch table for Jack and Ben and their staff of two girls. And one very late night, an autopsy was performed on this table by the doctors; on Ben's old dog Pat, who had died of mysterious causes.

The patient would be given a shot with a needle and syringe that had been sterilized in a silver bowl-like thing to be used and returned to be sterilized and used again. Due to their bulky size, Jack and Ben could carry only about six of these needles and syringes in their big, black medical bags. When they ran out, they had to go by the office to replenish their supply. For pregnant patients, the doctors listened to the baby's heartbeat with a fetoscope made up of a metal band around their foreheads and earphones. If they couldn't hear a heartbeat when they knew they should be able to, very often they would give up because their own hearts would be beating so loudly with anxiety that they could not distinguish between the two.

They were delivering approximately one hundred babies a year, which both Ben and Jack considered icing on the cake of general practice. It was monumentally time consuming but they loved it. Jack tells with great humor of the day in Woodford Memorial Hospital when he delivered one twin for his friend Dr. George Reed, raced to the other delivery room to deliver his own patient's baby, and came tearing back in time to deliver the second twin. He declares that the whole thing took less than ten minutes.

Sometime on really busy days at the office, a patient might be taken to a back room and forgotten for a while, as Jack says was the case with Ellen Cleveland. She had come in for an exam, and when he finally opened the door of the examining room to check her, she was on the table with her hat still planted firmly on her head calmly reading "The Saturday Evening Post." He never thinks of the old office without remembering Ellen and her hat.

Perhaps a more exciting morning came the day a father brought his daughter to the back door of the office saying he thought "she might be in labor." Ten minutes later, Ben delivered the baby in the back room amid great flurry. Mother and baby were fine. Ben and his nurse were fairly shaken.

The daily house calls provided the most insight into the lives of their patients and Jack and Ben have always thoroughly enjoyed making them. Sometimes they were harrowing, as in the time when Jack and the Episcopal Church Father were trying to talk a lady out of committing suicide with a loaded gun she had in her room. She tricked them into going out in the hall to wait for her, whereupon she slammed the door, locked the door, and loudly vowed to take her life. In his frustration, Jack pounded on the door to distract her while Father quietly climbed in a window and grabbed the gun without a shot being fired.

There were also times when home visits were funny, as was the case when the prominent, wealthy lady called Ben with minor symptoms wanting him to come out and check her. Ben promised to come out just as soon as he "could wind things up at the office." But he decided to detour by home to help grill steaks for the church group that he and Ruth were entertaining that night and, of course, he stayed long enough to hurriedly swallow his own steak dinner.

Upon arriving beside the lady's bed, he was ordered to sit at a small table while she had her butler bring him a full course dinner with soup, salad, main course, strawberry shortcake, the works. She told him that she felt sorry for him having to stay that late at the office and to work that hard, and Ben was left no option but to eat every bite with pretended gusto.

On the other hand, house calls for the doctors were sometimes incredibly sad, as Jack remembers was the situation when our good friend Bob Hicks was stricken with lung cancer at the age of forty-two. He was the ideal patient, never feeling sorry for himself, testing every 'cure' the doctors suggested, and trying mostly to put people at ease when they were around him. He was very ill the last three months and Jack never let a Sunday evening go by that he didn't run out to see Bob just to listen to his new symptoms, to reassure him whenever possible and to let him talk about his illness. It is the most devastating thing in a doctor's life to watch an incurable disease take its toll while all the medical training in the world can do nothing to alter the outcome. Bob died a courageous death on December 26th, 1967, in the Woodford Memorial Hospital and the entire community mourned its loss.

Woodford County Memorial Hospital provided Jack with his greatest challenge when we came to our new life in Midway. He had done his internship at Louisville General Hospital with all of updated technology and three hundred patient beds and he very nearly had a cultural shock when he first started on the staff of Woodford. The building itself had been a large, private home that had been converted to a thirty-five-bed hospital. There had been an addition in 1920 directly behind the home and a larger wing added in 1940, just behind the first addition. In the building that had been a home, there were two floors, a basement, a two-storied sun porch, and one elevator that had a grilled mesh door. The elevator was just large enough to hold one stretcher at a time provided the stretcher was turned catty-cornered.

There was a three-bed male ward on the first floor, a three-bed female ward on the second floor, and the rest were private rooms. One private room that had been a bedroom when the house had still been a home had a working fireplace. The sunporch downstairs was the business office, the upstairs porch served as a lounge for the patients. The emergency room was in the basement, along with the kitchen and doctor's lounge where they held staff meetings. There was one cook and one big black stove to provide all the food for the entire hospital. There was no dietary department, just one helper who brought the food up, and the nurses distributed it. The surgical ward was located in the 1940's wing, and it still is.

The hospital was staffed by seven general practitioners, one of whom had had a year or two of surgical training and did Cesareans, appendectomies, tonsillectomies, gall bladders and the like. His wife was a registered nurse, who had taken a course to be a nurse anesthetist and she worked with them during their surgeries. There were three surgeons and a bone specialist who would come if needed. The G.P.'s assisted on surgery, and this was terribly time consuming. Tonsillectomies were done with open drop ether, and often the doctors would get as much as the patients because the smell of ether would permeate the room as the anesthetist dropped it on the gauze that covered the face of the patient.

The hospital administrator and his wife were trained in nursing, and they would work the floor if the hospital was short on nurses. There was no such thing as a beeper and if the doctor had a pretty serious case in the hospital, he just had to stay near a phone. The funeral homes manned the only ambulances and I suppose they prospered from the business. There was a real feeling of comradery in the medical world of Woodford County in those days, and I believe the patients benefitted greatly from it.

There was also a good feeling in the town of Midway in 1959. Located in the heart of the Bluegrass Country of Kentucky, the town had been founded in 1833 by a railroad company and the tracks still ran down the middle of the business district of town. The streets were named for the railroad company's executives, and the shade trees that line every street were donated by one of these officials. There were approximately one thousand people living here in the 1960 census and the town measured about six blocks by four blocks.

The business area was small, with just a drug store, a bank, and a couple of grocery stores, hardware stores, and restaurants. One beautiful antique and gift shop was located up by the post office on Winter Street. It was owned and operated by the Lehman Family, a brother and two sisters, who were perhaps in their early fifties, and totally dedicated to the running of that wonderful business.

There was another Lehman brother, but he was in charge of several farms that they owned, and I never saw him in the shop. People came from miles around just to shop here, and to visit with the Lehmans. It was truly an institution. It was said that Midway was such a special place to live, and I always thought that it was the Lehman's Antique Shop that was at the heart of that uniqueness.

The post office, located in the same spot since 1917, was the social center of the day. Mail was not delivered to our homes. It still isn't. People looked forward to their daily treks to get their mail, to meet their friends and neighbors, and to find out 'the news'. Friends also met at the drug store bar stools and in the garage on US 421 where men went for coffee every morning.

Bridge at least once a week—with perhaps four tables participating and small prizes awarded, a bazaar and luncheon of chicken salad, oyster stew and homemade pies, given by the women of the Christian Church on the day before Thanksgiving, the Lion's Club Pancake Day held every election day from sunup until sundown. With the pancake batter coming from Weisenberger Mill just three miles down the road and a Fourth of July Picnic given by Bob and Niesje Hicks where about sixty of us would gather with our families at the farm, taking food and drink and enjoying their swimming pool in the afternoon sun, it is obvious that our social lives were unsophisticated and uncluttered. They centered around our churches our families and our neighbors. It was a good way to live.

There was very little air conditioning in Midway then, and people utilized their front porches in the evening to get cool, to speak to their neighbors and to sort of recap their day. It was a wonderful experience for me to walk the children after supper when Jack was gone on his home visits and get to know the townspeople. When the older ladies came to visit me, they wore white gloves and left calling cards on the table beside the door. This may sound pretentious now, but I found it to be utterly charming. They cared enough to make a visit an occasion and I loved it.

Outside the town limits, in every direction, were beautiful farms, mostly used in those days for cattle, tobacco and bluegrass seed with a few horse farms scattered in. These farms were often bordered to the front by the wonderful stone walls that were made by placing huge stones one on top of the other in such a way that they fit perfectly and would be standing one hundred years later without mortar to hold them in place as a testimony to the artistry of the men who built them. Narrow two-lane roads that ran from Midway in all four directions, one more lovely than the next.

There was a private school located here that was founded in 1847 by some of the men of the Christian Church, and it was intended to be a school for orphaned girls. By 1959, it had been enlarged to include girls from broken homes, foreign students and girls who just wanted an excellent education. The school then had grades seven through fourteen, the equivalent of two years of college, and the enrollment was approximately two hundred and fifty girls. Many of our social activities centered around the school's functions, and the people that came here to teach became some of our closest friends.

When we came initially, we agreed to stay a year, for Jack to find out how he liked being a country doctor, and for Ben to see if he wanted to work with Jack. We were overwhelmed by the beauty of the place, by the gentleness and caring of the people and by the joy that Jack experienced by practicing family medicine. Six weeks after we came, we decided that we'd probably never leave it. We were here to stay a lifetime, God willing.

PART TWO

The Interim Years

Ahead of the Hounds

1960-1963

He died for no reason a-tall...
> —Newell Hicks

The early days were hectic for Jack, as he was just learning the ropes. He rode everywhere in the county with Ben the first months trying to learn all the back roads and farms. One night he went alone to see a possible heart attack patient and drove around furiously for forty minutes unable to locate the farm, only to return to the hospital and find the man in the emergency room. They had been afraid to wait any longer. The next day Jack bought a detailed country map and he never left home without it.

Soon it became so chaotic at the office that they decided to start keeping appointments and they hired another girl. We lived in a little grey rental cottage on Stephens Street, and it was the usual thing for us to have several patients pounding on the door after dark every night of the week. Once when our bedroom backed up to the wall of the front porch and the head of our bed backed up to that wall on the inside, a man knocked at the front door after midnight. When Jack didn't get there right away, the man took his fist and beat against the wall just where my head was on the other side. I thought the house was falling down. I had never heard such a racket. Jack went quickly telling him that he would be right down to see the ailing wife and the man roared off in his old jalopy. We could hear the car tear around the block and come to stop again in front of our house.

"Hurry, Jack!" I said. "Get to the door before he hits the wall again!" But Jack was too late and the man whacked the wall with his fist in an effort to get Jack moving quicker. It worked.

The hospital went through an enormous change during these years as it received a great sum of money from two interested wealthy ladies. At last, part of the original dwelling house was demolished, and a larger, more fitting front was built. The new part included a large waiting room, an office, a doctor's lounge, and a cafeteria on the first floor. There were patient rooms on the second and third floors and with the contributions of a second lady, the entire floor was raised another level to accommodate a brand-new maternity ward. It was a major accomplishment, and the whole county took a great deal of pride in it.

Jack and Ben began talking to the architect who was doing the hospital and let him know that they were interested in building an office that would be more suitable for their needs. The present place was simply bursting at the seams. Property was so scarce in Midway that the two had no idea when a desirable location would ever become available, but they wanted to be ready should this opportunity occur, and they asked the architect to be drawing up some suggestions.

In the fall of 1960, Ben's Great-Aunt Lilly Parrish died and left her farm to Mr. Tom Roach, Ben's dad. When Mr.

Tom was eight years old, his mother had died, and he had been brought to live in the huge yellow brick house where his Uncle Jim and Aunt Lilly had no children, and they took care of Mr. Tom as if he were their own son. When the house and farm were left to him, Mr. Tom decided that he was too old to want to move from the old white frame house on Winter Street, and he insisted that Ben and Ruth go on up with their children to live. They gladly accepted and then they made their lovely Turner Street house available to us.

We loved our little grey house on Stephens Street, but it was on a busy street that leads out of town and our front yard was very small. We decided to take Ben and Ruth up on their offer as Turner Street was a dead-end street and their yard was enormous for the children to enjoy. In addition to this, Ben had always been interested in planting flowers, shrubs and trees, and their yard looked something like a page out of a magazine. We planned to move there during the first week of December.

At this point of our lives, Jack was gone almost all the time. It became necessary for me to develop interests of my own, or to run the risk of becoming homesick for family and friends back in Louisville. I joined a Garden Club to try to better understand how to care for the beautiful plants I had inherited from Ben. I hired a sitter once a week and would spend most of these free hours roaming around the Lehman's shop, learning by bits and pieces how to recognize "good" antiques, and how to know "periods" and "designs" they were so familiar to. And I became a big fan of the racetrack.

Mr. Tom was dabbling in the horses now and he had a few that he was actually racing, as well as several mares he was breeding. He loved racing and was very competitive although he never placed a bet to my knowledge. It was great fun for him to name his thoroughbreds and I remember a few of those names. "Orterdo" was named for Mrs. Roach, as she always said that she "orterdo" one thing or another. "Midway Mayor" was for his friend Howard Rouse, "Constant Critic" for Mrs. Roach again. "Widow's Walk" named for all the widows on Winter Street and "Red Jonelle" for me, as I have red hair.

Having Mr. Tom name a race horse for me was one of the greatest joys of my life. Jack and I drove around to Cincinnati, Louisville, and Lexington often with him to see that horse run. The best she ever did was come in fifth, I guess we'd have gone crazy if she had ever won a race! I realized that I was probably going to the races more than I should on the day I told Jenny I was excited because I had won the door prize at the Lions Club Dinner the night before and she asked innocently, "Which horse was you ridin', Mom?"

Mr. Tom had become terribly important to our entire family, and he was always the first to arrive on Christmas morning with presents for each child. He came to visit us all year, once or twice a week to watch the children play for an hour or so while he told me stories of Midway. My favorite yarn of his involved Newell Hicks, our neighbor and veterinarian, when he was a schoolboy. It seems that one of his school projects was to carefully watch a pet lamb and to write down the lamb's progress every day in a notebook. On the final page of the report, Newell had scribbled the words, "He died for no reason a-tall."

Mr. Tom had many delightful, humorous stories and he repeated them so often that I thought I'd never forget any of them. It's incredibly sad to me that most of them have faded from memory and now only the feeling that I would get while sitting and listening to this kind and gentle man is still as sharp and poignant as it was over twenty years ago.

It was in the spring of 1962 that a lot became available for the possible site for a new doctor's office building and the location was perfect. The only problem with the whole thing was that there was a thirteen-room former boarding house standing on the lot and the asking price was just about four times what Jack and I were hoping to spend. Added to this, the owners demanded that the buyers come up with an additional four thousand dollars to buy all the furniture that was left after the family had taken all they wanted. This pushed Jack and me over the edge, and we said that we couldn't go that extra amount. At this point Mr. Tom stepped in and declared that if it would help us all out, he would buy the furniture and would sell it at auction on the day we would be selling the old house. It had been our idea all along to sell the building at auction to anyone willing to dismantle it and to clear the lot for us within two months. This was the way the whole thing was settled.

On a hot Saturday morning in August 1962, Ben and Ruth were out of town and Jack was tied up at the office. Mr. Tom and I went down for the big sale. We watched helplessly as the big Old House went for the first and only bid of twenty-five dollars, and all the furniture went for less than two thousand. We were both big losers, but we managed an embarrassed laugh about it and agreed that at least we had removed the barriers and now the building could begin.

The design of the office was going to cause trouble because Ben was flamboyant and modern, and Jack was plain and traditional. They had agreed on a floor plan, using Ben's brother-in-law's office design that had proven excellent in Atlanta. The part that was going to cause trouble was the exterior, the look about the place. Several plans had to be abandoned by both Jack and Ben, until finally there was a compromise by both and on Feb. 7th, 1963, the ground was broken with a shovel that had been hastily painted gold.

In December of that year, Jack and Ben held an open house in the new building and people came from miles around to see it. From the beginning it had seemed to be a community effort, and there was a grand sense of accomplishment felt on all sides to see the final result. Compliments abounded along with a general feeling of good will. It was with great expectations that the doors opened for service during the week of Christmas 1963.

PHOTO GALLERY

Ben and Jack looking at medical chart

Ben and Jack in the field of Ben's farm (which became Parrish Hill).
Baby Matt Fisher on Ben's shoulder.

Our first home in Midway on Stephens Street

Ben, Jack, and Mr. Les Pruitt (builder of office) on office site with a shovel painted gold.

Jack, Pat Fehrs, Ruth, Mom Fisher, Jo and Ben

Mid sixties Hicks' July 4th yearly family picnic-swim on their farm

Ben at bat in summer competition at the Midway school baseball field

Bruce Davis, Jack, Pat Davis and Jo

Ben with Nancy Bowling of Darien, Connecticut and Ann T. Fisher at the
Kentucky Derby.

At Airdrie Farm on Old Frankfort Pike, families gathered for a seven degree temperature fabulous big sled pulled by a tractor driven by Mr. Carl Lathrem.

Alex Alexander with Jo at the Frontier Nursing Hospital, Eastern Kentucky, 1977.

Mr. Tom Roach who died in September, 1975

Family photo made in the 1960's; Jenny, Matt, Peter, Jo, Jack, Ann T.

PART THREE

The Journals

*We all know something is eternal. And it ain't houses and it ain't names, and it ain't earth, and it ain't even the stars...
Everybody knows in their bones that something is eternal, and that something has to do with human beings.*
—*Our Town*, Act III, by Thornton Wilder

Ahead of the Hounds

1964

—A Few Figs from Thistles
Edna St. Vincent Millay
(Quoted by Ben's Aunt Des)

JANUARY 3RD

Mom Fisher drove up for lunch with the boys today and we couldn't wait for Jack. He came in at three p.m. for lunch and didn't leave the office for the day until eight–twenty tonight. It's a good thing nobody said it would be easy.

JANUARY 5TH

Tonight, we went to Bill and Jerry Taylor's for supper. He is the Christian Church minister and Ben, Ruth, Dick and Hilda Starks, Jim and Sarah Raisor, Hub and Tempa Endicott were all there. Jerry had fixed wild goose and country ham. A feast!

After supper we played twelve-handed Hearts, which was unruly to say the least. Ruth won for the night and Jack lost the most. Great fun.

JANUARY 8TH

Jack took over as President of the Woodford County Medical Association today and is very proud of the honor.

JANUARY 9TH

A lady slipped and fell in the waiting room at the new office today and broke her hip. We are not sure whether our old insurance covers the new building or not, or if our builder is still liable because the building isn't finished. Sure hope she doesn't sue. Jack says she is a nice old lady but she was in the office to be examined after an injury sustained while riding on a train, trying to decide whether to sue the railroad. Sounds ominous.

JANUARY 18TH

The lady has decided to sue Roach and Fisher, we are not sure of the amount yet.

JANUARY 19TH

Ben's Great-Aunt Des Parrish was terribly sick today. She's an inspiration to two or three younger generations. Earlier this week when Jack was at the hospital in the middle of the night, he saw her light on and stuck his head in her door. He found her reading a book and asked her if she didn't think she should be sleeping. She quoted the famous Edna St. Vincent Millay lines to him:

My candle burns at both ends
It will not last the night;
But, ah, my foes, and oh, my friends—
It gives a lovely light.

Jack closed the door and left her to her reading.

JANUARY 21ST

Miss Des was buried today with a very private funeral. This is a real loss to all of Midway.

JANUARY 23RD

Ben and Jack have started a program to help the University medical school by taking one senior student at a time and teaching him his general practice rotation. There will be no recompence for this as they both feel that this is a contribution they should make. The first student is there now and will stay with them for several weeks.

JANUARY 30TH

I had the office staff down to lunch today, and the student came along. He is a really funny boy. The girls were teasing him because yesterday after lunch, they heard a horrendous crash in the back examining room. They went tearing back and found him sprawled out on the floor. He had climbed up on an examine table to take a nap, fallen asleep and had promptly rolled off causing the ruckus.

FEBRUARY 3RD

The girls called for me to work at the office today, as they were swamped, and I can at least answer the phones for them.

The two doctors saw seventy-four patients and we were all exhausted by the end of the day. I came home at seven, Jack at eight-thirty, then he had to go to the hospital. It is now ten-thirty, and I am going to bed even though he has not come home yet.

FEBRUARY 6TH

We showed a young doctor through the office tonight, trying to interest him in coming into the practice. Ben and Jack simply must have some relief.

FEBRUARY 20TH

Matt was five today! We all came downstairs together, and he was appropriately thrilled with the toys and wagon. Jack read a book to the children while I fixed breakfast, and it was all pretty great. Although it was his day off, Jack had to spend the afternoon at the hospital. When he had not come in at six-thirty, he called and told me to go and take the kiddos to the Christian Church chili supper without him. We sat with Mr. Tom.

FEBRUARY 21ST

Jack told me tonight that Ben, Mr. Tom, and Bud Greeley are really going into the horse business seriously come June. I hate to see it happen because it is bound to interfere with Ben's time at the office, but I know it is what he wants.

MARCH 1ST

Jack got a call at seven-forty-five this morning saying there was a wreck on the Versailles Road, and he was needed. Jack went running out but by the time he arrived on the spot, the seventeen-year-old boy was dead, and his brother (fifteen years old) was in terrible shape. Jack sent him to the University Hospital, and I drove Jack up tonight to see the boy.

MARCH 2ND

Talked to Ruth a while this morning. The cost of the new office will tally up to be $65,656.28. More than we were expecting, to say the least. Jack and I went over the invoices during his lunchtime.

MARCH 5TH

Ben and Ruth came down later tonight and we went over the builder's bid. We found a few very minor mistakes, so it'll probably be the $65,000.00.

MARCH 7TH

We went to the Woodford County High School Basketball tournament game with Ben and Ruth. It was an exciting game, but we lost to Frankfort. Afterwards, we went to their house to play cards, and Ben's farm hand came in for help in delivering a calf. We ran out to the barn, and Ruth and I watched while Ben and Jack tried to help. Jack had a terrible expression on his face the entire time.

MARCH 13TH

About twenty people went with Jack and me tonight up to Ben and Ruth's for a chili supper and bridge. Last month the Girls School gave a chili supper which we all attended, and the chili was not good. Several of us did not feel well the next day and we blamed it on the chili. Well, Ruth bought what was left over, froze it, and invited us up for another round of it and to play bridge. All week I had teased, Jim Raisor and Dick Starks about having one week to save their stomachs as well as their souls by joining the Catholic Faith as we could not eat meat on Fridays. I told Ruth that we could come for bridge, but couldn't eat the chili, but she insisted we come for the entire evening saying she would be glad to whip up something meatless for us.

Needless to say, the friends didn't join the faith and when we all sat down, everyone was served the chili except Jack and me. We were served frozen fish dinners, and I do mean frozen, because they had never been defrosted. I guess it had been forgotten to run them in the oven or forgotten to turn on the oven. Anyway, Don Johnson served them very carefully to us with huge hot-pads, so he had no idea of knowing that they were literally ice cold. I bit down on the peas first, thank God, and it was like eating crushed ice. I didn't dare look at Jack across the table, because I knew we would burst out laughing. I managed to eat the peas by holding them in my mouth until they melted enough to swallow, and I positively devoured the delicious salad and dessert. Jack ate nearly all his dinner, then placed his empty salad plate on top of his dinner plate to hide all that was left. I couldn't talk to anyone at the table because I was on the verge of hysterical laughter. Jim and Dick will have the last laugh because the chili was perfectly delicious. This just goes to prove that you can't trust Friday the thirteenth.

MARCH 18TH

Jack and Ben took the office staff and their husbands and Ruth and me to a Lexington night spot for dinner, and it was fun. Ben was dancing with Maxine Gilkerson when he pretended to see her Baptist minister come in. She ducked her head and belted from the door before realizing he was pulling her leg.

He told the story about the night he and Ruth thought they heard someone in their house after they had gone to bed. They didn't do anything about it, just hoping they were mistaken, and the noise would go away. The next day at the office, a man came in to see Ben. He was a noted town alcoholic and he said, "Where was you last night Doc? I came in your house looking for you, but I couldn't find you anyplace." We all concluded that we are going to have to start locking doors.

MARCH 23RD

Ben came down to talk to Jack about the Practice, and we had some lemonade. Nothing was decided. The lady who fell in the office has had a change of heart and is not going to sue!

MARCH 27TH

An old fellow fell in his yard in Versailles this morning with a ruptured abdominal aorta, so Jack, Ben, Dick Crutcher (surgeon) and an anesthesiologist stayed in the operating room from from ten in the morning until five-thirty in the afternoon, repairing the aorta. The surgery was a success, but the patient died, they think of a heart attack. Jack was exhausted tonight, really tense. We ate late supper and took a very long walk.

APRIL 4TH

Jack and I went to the races at Keeneland today with Mr. Tom to see his new horse "Orterdo" run in the first race. It was a photo for second place, was awarded third, paying only three dollars and eighty cents. As we had it across the board, we collected only our ticket for the day.

APRIL 9TH

Jack was track physician at Keeneland today, and it was a lovely day. We cashed one six-dollar ticket between us, but we managed to enjoy the whole affair.

APRIL 15TH

Jenny, Matt, the office girls, Jack, and I went to Keeneland today to see Ben's horse, "Promwood" run in the Thoroughbred Club Dinner race. It ran dead last, and I felt sorry for Ben having us all there.

APRIL 30TH

Jack's "day off" but he didn't come in until two this afternoon. He had a quick lunch and was called back immediately to the hospital to deliver two babies. He finished both and came rolling in just five minutes late to pick up our four guests and we headed over to Beaumont Inn for supper.

MAY 13TH

My brother-in-law, Jim Bowling, was visiting here for the Girls' Schools Trustees Meeting and needed to catch the late afternoon train out of town. As it usually doesn't stop, I asked John Willie McDaniel, our policeman to help us flag it down. It ended with half the people of Midway standing by the tracks, curious as to why John Willie was stopping the train, and why this patrol car had its red top light going around and all of us waving like crazy when the train appeared. Jim came to the back of the train after he had boarded and waved his hat to the crowd as he took off. He looked like a political contender.

MAY 22ND

Jenny fell from the monkey bar in the back yard and broke her arm. I was frantic and Jack had just left for a weekend church retreat and I had no idea where Ben might be. Warley Harper, our back-door neighbor, took Matt with him and drove around until he found Ben making a house call, and we soon had things taken care of. Ben missed a dinner party in order to take Jenny and me to the hospital in Lexington to have the arm set. Ben and Warley were both very good friends for folks in need.

Ben has named a racehorse for Jack! He is calling it "Good Old Jack."

MAY 25TH

Jack was seeing one of his OB's today and he was tired as it was late in the afternoon. The girl had trouble with swelling in her ankles and feet and she was telling him about it. He looked up from her chart where he had been reading and asked, "Just when did your feet begin to smell?" Lucky for him she had a great sense of humor.

JUNE 5TH

I spent the entire morning trying to get our office loan that we have with Ben switched over to the bank. I am not good with money, but Jack is terrible and has turned everything financial over to me. The switch to the bank was quite involved as Ben had to co-sign our note. We now owe the Midway Bank and Trust thirty-six thousand dollars, and it scares me to death.

JULY 4TH

Jack came in at lunchtime and we took off with the kids for the Hicks' pool. Every Fourth of July about sixty people gather out there, bringing their own meat, drinks, and one dish and we have a wonderful picnic by the swimming pool. It is a great day, and we look forward to it every year. We had to come home early this year because Jack had to go to the hospital.

JULY 5TH

The Fisher Clan came up for the day and stayed for supper. After lunch we all walked up to Mr. Tom's orchard to get apples. I have never seen them so abundant as this year.

JULY 16TH

They called for me to help out at the office again and I was there by nine-thirty. It was a wild morning with Jack gone to National Guard camp, three real emergencies popping in, and Ben with appointments absolutely every fifteen minutes. Ruth worked the afternoon, and I went back at four and stayed until Ben finished at seven.

I hurried home, picked up Jenny and Matt, took the sitter home, and made it in time to the Christian Church ice cream supper. We sat with Mr. Tom.

JULY 25TH

Jack came home Friday and has been as busy as a bird dog ever since. I think he missed the practice—he has been eager to work this weekend.

AUGUST 4TH

The family went to the Pink Pig for supper to celebrate my thirty-first birthday. Jenny and Matt gave me China dogs from the drugstore that they had dropped on the way home. Both had broken front legs—I think I can glue them back.

AUGUST 7TH

Ambrose Preston came to the office complaining to Jack that she had coughed all night. He asked her if she had taken anything for it, and she timidly said that upon finding nothing better in the house to use, she had rubbed her chest down with Listerine. They both laughed until they cried.

AUGUST 9TH

Beautiful Sunday. Jack came in at noon so we ate quickly and headed to the Kentucky River and Ben's boat. Mistake. We went up the river, thank God, and Jack swam while I read the paper. Then we both read books while soaking up the sun. We started home around four o'clock and the motor was as dead as a door mat. As we were upstream, we were able to drift all the way down, but it took hours. Extremely frustrating, but there was nothing to do but drift. We were very late getting home.

SEPTEMBER 10TH

We have decided to name the baby either Peter Garrett for Jack's great grandfather or Ann Thompson, for my sister and Mr. Tom, whose full name is Thompson Marcus Roach.

OCTOBER 8TH

Jack's day off but he worked most of the afternoon. He went to an inspection of the National Guard last night with Bill Buster and came home at midnight. Up at four for an OB—and it was a breach—Mongoloid, a real problem, but she finally delivered.

OCTOBER 25TH

We went to the Pink Pig last night with Matt and Jenny for chili and pie. I woke up at midnight sure the labor had begun. Around four-fifteen, I called Jack—we phoned Jim Raisor to come over to stay with the children and we took off for the Baptist Hospital in Lexington. Peter Garrett was born at six-forty-two a.m. He was eight pounds, four ounces, and was twenty-one inches long! He was bald! Ben came up to check him out immediately and reported that he was completely normal and everything was wonderful in this best of all possible worlds.

NOVEMBER 1ST

We came home from the hospital two days ago, and Peter had rubbed all the skin off his nose, prompting Mr. Tom to say he looked like he had been in a fight. When Matt finally worked up the nerve to sidle over to see his baby brother, he was aghast that Peter did not have any teeth. Mr. Tom's present to Peter was five shiny silver dollars delivered in a plaid tobacco draw-string bag.

NOVEMBER 13TH

I went down to Bett Weisenberger's house this afternoon for a cup of tea. We used to visit back and forth for tea regularly, but this was the first time since Peter had arrived. Her sister in Louisville had lent me several beautiful maternity dresses and I had boxed them up to mail back, but I wasn't sure of her address. When I asked Bett she answered with a little agitation, "Leave them here. I will take care of them."

"Oh, I can't do that Bett. It is a chore to mail anything. Just give me her address," I persisted.

"Leave them here," she repeated with an emphasis that was unusual for Bett and when I looked closely, I could tell that her face was a little flushed.

"Bett," I asked, "Are you going to need to wear these clothes?" She finally grinned a little and admitted sheepishly that that was exactly the case.

Ahead of the Hounds

1967

I thought you were Jenny's Mommy. Are you just the cook?
—Six-year-old Jamie

JANUARY 1ST

Can't believe it has been two years since I last wrote in my journal. I will try to get back on it this year—that is one of my resolutions.

Jack has hospitalized old Mrs. McCauley because she fell at Taylor Manor and broke her hip. She has become very senile but has been happy in her senility so it isn't as bad as it could be. Anyway, flowers were pouring into the hospital from her friends and family, and she told the nurses that they were for her wedding. When they asked her who the lucky groom might be, she smiled and said, "Why Dr. Fisher, of course."

JANUARY 20TH

Last week Bob Hicks came in to see Jack, as he was due to go out west to a meeting and he had been unable to get rid of a cough and congestion. Jack did routine x-rays of the chest, and there was a spot on one lung as big as a silver dollar. Jack sent him directly up to Dr. Dick Crutcher, fearing that it was a malignancy. Dr. Crutcher's opinion was the same as Jack's and we are all devastated. Bob is a wonderful human being—warm, kind, and generous. I cannot bear to think what this could mean. Bob is only forty-two years old.

JANUARY 25TH

Bob has had the surgery on his lung and our worst fears have been confirmed. Dr. Crutcher removed the lobe of his lung, and he seems to be doing very well. They think we have every reason to be optimistic.

JANUARY 28TH

Jack received a wonderful letter from a patient today. The last paragraph read: *The manner in which you live your life and contribute to humanity makes you one of the most admired and respected people in my life.*

This letter came at a good time. Jack is feeling pretty low about medicine in general and himself in particular. Lung cancer is a horrible thing for a doctor to confront in any circumstance, but it is almost intolerable when the patient is such a good friend as Bob Hicks.

FEBRUARY 10TH

One of the men who worked for the Lehmans died of a heart attack. As it was very sudden, it was quite a shock for the family. His brother-in-law, who has something very wrong with his eyes in that when one is looking directly at you, the other eye tends to wander. He came by our house to pick up a "yellow jacket" pill for his sister who was hysterical over the death of her husband. I gave him the pill Jack had left for him and told him I was so sorry about the death in his family. He looked at me, grinned a broad grin, shrugged his shoulders, and uttered the profound statement, "Oh, well. Here today, gone tomorrow." I did not have an answer.

MARCH 3RD

Ben had an unusual thing happen in the office last week. He was seeing a lady that he liked, and she told him that she had left a country ham on the back seat of his car, and she hoped that he and Ruth would enjoy it. When he went home for lunch, he reached in the back seat of his car for the ham and it was not there. He called Ruth to ask if she had picked up the ham at the office. She knew nothing about the ham.

All of a sudden, he remembered seeing a ne'er-do-well fellow loitering around the back of the office when he had come to work that morning. He felt sure that this man must have made off with the ham. He called John Willie and told him that he did not want this man arrested but would he please go and bring his ham back.

John Willie was able to locate the fellow right away and he questioned him back and forth for a long time, with the man denying the theft every step of the way. The poor man is known to be a ne'er-do-well, but he had never been thought of as a thief, so John Willie finally believed his story, and had come back to Ben empty handed. Ben was really upset but decided there just wasn't much else he could do about it.

Early the next morning the phone rang at the office, and it was a lady patient that Ben had seen the day before. She told him that she had gone out to the garage a few minutes ago and had discovered a package on the back seat. It was a beautiful country ham and she couldn't imagine where in the world it had come from. Finally, it had dawned on her that her car was exactly like Ben's, and as she had parked in the back of the office the day before very close to Ben's car, she wondered if possibly the ham might have been meant for him. Everybody got a big laugh out of the improbable situation— except possibly the poor ne'er-do-well.

MAY 24TH

At high noon yesterday, Ann Thompson Fisher came into this world weighing in at seven pounds, eight ounces, and she was nineteen inches long. Jack ran by to see Mr. Tom to ask him if we might call the baby's name "Thompson" after him, and he said he was delighted to have a little girl namesake. That he had a couple of old boys named for him, but never a pretty little girl, and he would be honored. The "Ann" is for my sister.

AUGUST 16TH

The rich little Albercrombie boys from Midway Farm out on the Versailles Road, (there are two…Jamie, aged six and Georgie, aged four) spent the day here yesterday so their Nanny could have her hair fixed. As a favor to her, I stayed with them all day reading stories to them as well as to Jenny and Matt. I did not want them to get hurt in any way, so I played games too. I did want them to have a good time.

They wanted bacon and tomato sandwiches for lunch and as I started to fry the bacon, I noticed Jamie leaning against the kitchen door with a look of sheer disappointment on his face. I asked what in the world was the matter and he replied, "I thought you were Jenny's mommy. Are you just the cook?"

SEPTEMBER 12TH

Ben and Jack have hired two new girls for their staff, and they are great. The doctors have been so lucky with their nurses—they all get along so well with the patients and with each other and they really do get the job done. There was one time when their choice for a new nurse misfired, and this was with a girl that Ben called Dolly. She was young and blonde with beautiful blue eyes. The first day she came to work she wore a tight fitting red dress and three and a half inch heels. The staff was suspicious.

Dolly was friendly enough and seemed harmless until they found out that she had given a number of children the measle vaccine dilutant without the vaccine. These people all had to be called back to be given a lame excuse and another inoculation —this one was free.

It was about this time that our Peter was due his six-week checkup and DPT shot, and I was determined that Dolly would not be doing the shooting. I called the office to make an appointment with Ben on a day when Maxine would be working with him, and I thought I had covered the bases. But in spite of my precautions, after Ben finished the exam, Dolly breezed in with a needle and said she was to give the shot, which she did on the spot. I was wild when Ben slipped into the room as I was dressing Peter and admitted that she had given a wrong shot to my baby. Luckily, it was the adult DT which is weaker than the Pediatric injection, so no harm was done.

To our great relief, Dolly left shortly after that, and we thought we had seen the last of her. Then Ben received a letter from a respected nurse anesthetist school asking for a recommendation for her, as she wanted to pursue this nursing specialty. Ben wrote back an adamant letter saying she was very careless, and scatter brained and definitely had no place in anesthesiology. It was to our great surprise and dismay that soon after that, she turned up at Woodford Memorial with her accreditation and ready to go to work.

To bring this affair full circle round, Ben had to have a hernia operation. He called on his friend Dick Crutcher to do the surgery and strongly stressed that he did not want to be put to sleep—especially by Dolly. And to please do the job with a local anesthetic. Dick agreed that this would be proper.

A few days later Ben was lying on a stretcher in Woodford Hospital waiting to be taken to the operating room. He looked up and saw Dolly standing over him with a smile on her face and a needle in her hand. Before he could voice a protest, she jammed the needle into his arm, and he remembered nothing else.

When Dick came into surgery, he exclaimed that Ben had requested not to be put to sleep. Dolly then volunteered to wake him back up, whereupon Dick responded, "Don't do that! We will all be better off now if he sleeps through this."

Miraculously Ben recovered, and Dolly's husband was soon transferred from the county. You couldn't hope for a better ending than that.

SEPTEMBER 15TH

Bob Hicks has been having terrible pain in his hip. We are despondent as Jack thinks it is probably cancer spread. Frequently it pops up in other places. Jack says that he does not like the sound of it. If this turns out to be so, the prognosis is grim.

DECEMBER 26TH

Bob Hicks is dead. I never knew a more courageous man. He met a terrible death head-on and managed never to lose his dignity. He set an example for us all.

We came back from Louisville early yesterday and went straight to the hospital to see Bob. He was too weak to be able to drink from a straw and he was thirsty. Jack cut the straw to about three inches and Bob could drink from that. Even under these circumstances, he summoned up a grin of thanks to Jack.

It was unbearably sad to see him like that. For the rest of my life, I will always remember Bob's death at Christmastime.

DECEMBER 30TH

A couple of days ago we had just come in from Bob Hick's funeral and we were utterly depleted. We were sitting at the kitchen table drinking coffee and trying to get ahold of ourselves. Bud Walden came in and announced that his family had decided to sell the beautiful lot across Turner Street, and they were willing to sell it to us for a reasonable price. Under any other circumstance, we would have been jubilant, as we had been looking for a suitable place to build a house for at least five years. But because of our despair over Bob, we did not want to talk about it right then. The land just didn't seem important to us in comparison with our human relationships on that particular day.

Ahead of the Hounds

1968

No, it won't keep me awake, but it'll help.

—Honeywood Rouse

MARCH 23RD

We are staying at Beaumont Inn in Harrodsburg for a little R&R. We are in the process of drawing up plans for a house we want to build, starting in September. Jack left five overdue OB cases, planning on tearing back the thirty miles to the hospital should anyone go into labor. But by night seven inches of snow had fallen—the most in March in Harrodsburg for eighty-one years. It is incredibly beautiful but will be a problem for Jack should he have to be back in a hurry.

MARCH 24TH

After dinner of wonderful country ham and fried chicken at the Inn, we played Bingo in the large parlor with the other guests here—two older couples, three older ladies, a middle-aged couple with their son (a smart aleck) and another young couple. The first prize was a jar of red raspberry preserves, which I won. The evening was over at nine-thirty.

MARCH 27TH

Labe Jackson called tonight for Jack saying his wife's father had died and she needed a sedative to sleep. When Jack went, Carol refused medication, saying that it was her father, and it was right for her to be upset. A bright sensitive girl. I like her.

APRIL 17TH

Ben and Ruth came down to play cards and he got to laughing about the night that a gentleman had died, and the family called Ben and the Catholic priest to come. They wanted Ben to pronounce the man legally dead, and the priest to administer last rites. The priest believed that last rites had to precede the official death pronouncement in order to be valid, so he raced past Ben, who was going up the steps of the home when he arrived. The priest was carrying his cloth, candles, holy oil, etc., and he tore in the house ahead of Ben who had to wait in the hall until the priest completed the ritual which lasted quite a long time.

MAY 1ST

Mr. Tom now keeps suckers in his pockets, and when he sees children, he gives them one. The children go wild when they see him—they adored him even before the suckers.

MAY 13TH

Sunday Jack was Master of Ceremonies at the dedication of the new wing at the Taylor Manor Nursing Home. It was quite an honor for him.

MAY 23RD

We celebrated Ann Thompson Fisher's first birthday this afternoon, and all fourteen children that live in the block that surrounds our back yard were on hand. Mr. Tom arrived, bringing her another one-hundred-dollar check to be put away for her education. He has been wonderful to Ann T saying it is so special for him to have a girl named for him.

MAY 29TH

We are going to choose our lighting fixtures for our new house next Wednesday up at Lehman's with Miss Elizabeth and I dread it. I stand in such awe of her anyway—can't imagine disagreeing with her choices, whether we like them or not. She called me up to her house today to show me her cutting board top on her kitchen cabinet, her narrow cabinet for tray storage, and her hardware on her doors. She had cut out articles for me to read—it was just great for her to take such an interest.

MAY 31ST

Worked in the yard today and cut my first roses. I took three buds to Miss Mayme Cogar and Miss Honeywood Rouse was visiting there. Miss Honeywood will be seventy tomorrow, Miss Mayme is ninety-one. I love the story about Miss Honeywood when she was at a party and asked for a cup of coffee. As it was getting pretty late, the hostess said, "But Honeywood, won't it keep you awake?"

"No, it won't keep me awake," Honeywood answered. "But it'll help."

JUNE 5TH

Miss Elizabeth and Joe assisted us in choosing our lights and our hardware today. They are so knowledgeable and are wonderful to take the time to help us.

We have bought a little brown, fourteen-foot run-about boat with a forty-horsepower motor, and we put it in the water at Frankfort today. Jack is like a child with a new toy, and I know it will be a great get-away for him. We had a picnic to celebrate and spent the afternoon in the sun.

JUNE 7TH

The children and I came home from shopping in Lexington and headed to Hick's pool to swim. It is impossible to go to that farm without thinking about Bob and remembering how wonderful he was. He used to drive an old beat-up station wagon that had a loose front door on the driver's side, that would swing open when Bob rounded a corner. He would reach out and grab it, slam it shut and with a huge grin on his face, wave to you with the same motion. Lung cancer is a horrible thing. I miss him. He has been dead almost six months, and I still expect to see him when I turn into that farm.

JUNE 9TH

Jack was on duty at the hospital this weekend and was gone night and day. I am glad that duty just comes once every two months. Tomorrow is City Council for him.

JUNE 12TH

We spent the day on the Kentucky River in our boat and had a great time. We swam around awhile then Jack skied, the kids drove the boat a little under close supervision, and we were home by four.

Mr. Tom celebrated his seventy-eighth birthday, and we took him a key holder and a picture of Ann T. He has started calling her Ann T and somehow it has caught on with all of us.

JULY 14TH

Jean and Ike Rouse asked us to go to Shakertown for dinner tonight and the Eysters asked us for bridge and dinner, but Jack had a difficult OB, and we didn't go anywhere, I stayed home and sewed and yelled at the kids.

AUGUST 6TH

Jimmy Stone and Windy Sharon, the men who are to build our house, came down last night with crushing news that our house will cost between sixty and sixty-five thousand dollars. That is astronomical for us now, and we will have to consider serious cuts.

AUGUST 9TH

Picked up the detailed specifications for the house today and over wine and a good meal at the Ramada Inn in Frankfort, we went over the thing letter by letter. We decided to cut wherever we can without bleeding, and to let her roll.

AUGUST 22ND

This afternoon was at least ninety-seven degrees and not a leaf moving. I took a cold salad to the people that have moved into Miss Mayme's house. She fell and broke her hip, and it didn't heal properly. She is unable to walk and had to go to Taylor Manor Nursing Home for the rest of her life. She told her nephew, James, to sell the house and all that is in it for whatever price he could get. The Evans Family was driving through town looking for a place to buy, saw the sign, made the deal, and moved in bag and baggage. Miss Mayme asked James to buy a good bottle of wine and set out two of her best wine glasses on the little table in the living room for the Evans parents to enjoy on the first night in their new home. She is quite an incredible lady.

AUGUST 31ST

Our neighbor, Lucy Bethel Holt, had to go to the hospital yesterday because she had a pain in her chest and was congested. Jack did routine tests on her and last night he went over her x-rays. There on her lung, as big as a golf ball, was a spot exactly where Bob Hick's had been. Both Jack and the radiologist think it is malignant. She was Bob's aunt and completely devoted to him—it was so hard on her to see him die last year, and now it will be doubly hard on her to have to face this again so soon after. Jack has gone now to tell her and ask her to go to Lexington to be under a surgeon's care. She has always said that she would never allow herself to be operated on for cancer, and I really doubt she will. She doesn't have anyone terribly close to her as she never married. Wish I could help her.

SEPTEMBER 4TH

Lucy Bethel agreed to go to Lexington for further tests, and last night Dr. Crutcher called Jack in agreement with his diagnosis of lung cancer. There is no way to know without surgery and she forbids that. Dr. Crutcher says that with her heart, she could not do on one lung, so it would mean just a lobe removed like Bob. She is gambling for time.

SEPTEMBER 9TH

Saturday night we went with Ben and Ruth to take Jim and Ann Gay to dinner and Jack and Ben are interested in taking him into the practice as a partner in June, and I must say Jack and I were impressed. Jim didn't say yes, but he didn't say no. Jack is on the City Council now and they are meeting tonight.

SEPTEMBER 16TH

Jack was supposed to go to the Civil War Round Table tonight at six o'clock, but he called at seven-thirty saying he was still at the office. And all I had for him to eat was chicken soup and hamburger. He is back at the office now and it's eleven forty-five p.m.

SEPTEMBER 18TH

Jimmy Stone and Windy Sharon came last night and their final bid on the house, after all cuts, was $57,500.00. We said, "Begin!" It is so much higher than we wanted, but what can you do. From all appearances, things are going even higher.

SEPTEMBER 22ND

Lucy Bethel told me that Ben had convinced her to have her lung operation and it is set up for next Wednesday. I believe this is what she wanted all along—to be talked into it.

SEPTEMBER 26TH

Lucy Bethel was operated on this morning and seemed to be doing OK. They removed the lower left lobe and some nodules. I don't know yet what that means. Windy came by—they are staking the house tomorrow. He just put a big sign on the property which says, "Sharon and Stone—Fisher Job" in big sort of crude hand painted letters. I love it.

SEPTEMBER 28TH

Had to go see the doctor today for my yearly checkup and when I got home, they had broken ground for the house! A red-letter day!! Jack and I have been married for twelve years and this is our very first house to own. It is going to be fantastic living just across the street from the building where I will see every nail go in.

I had a clean bill of health from Dr. Edger.

OCTOBER 3RD

We went to Ben and Ruth's last night to celebrate their twenty-fifth anniversary and their four children gave them a tandem bike.

OCTOBER 17TH

The student ate lunch with us—he is a great guy. He told the amazing story that had happened to him at the University

Hospital. He said they were treating a little old lady obviously terminal with cancer, when the students decided not to draw blood every day, but, for her comfort, every other day. When the resident approached her bed to check her with his students, he glanced at her chart and demanded in a loud voice, "Why wasn't blood drawn this morning? How is this omission going to look at death conference?"

The student said the little old lady shrank deeper in the bed and got an awful look on her face. Whereupon the resident patted her arm and hurriedly said, "There, there, don't you worry about a thing. Everything's going to be alright." The students stood by appalled.

OCTOBER 20TH

The trouble started today because we had too much on the agenda. Jack wanted to get the boat out of the water for the winter, but Jenny and Matt wanted to go to Rhodes Ingerton's tenth birthday party. So, Jack took Peter with him to the river, and I stayed home with Ann T to take the group to the party and to be at the dock in Frankfort at five o'clock sharp with the boat hitch and trailer to pick up the boat riders.

Everything was going according to schedule, and I was in Frankfort with Baby Ann T just on time. The traffic was horrendous, and I had to go through mobs of people and cars, pulling the awkward boat trailer, and being very careful about turns. We learned later that there was some traffic disorder around the college and the police were out in force. The taillight wasn't working properly on the trailer, and this added to my disorder as this was against the law.

We were there at the appointed time, and we waited. At six o'clock I phoned some people we know at Clifton Boat Dock, and they had not seen Jack. At six-fifteen Ann T was screaming with hunger, so we had to head home through the riots again, still pulling the empty, tail-lightless trailer. I fed her a plain butter sandwich and changed her diaper. The phone rang and I grabbed it up. It was Jack at our friends' house in Clifton and he did not seem too upset. He had had boat trouble, couldn't get the motor going, but finally it had turned over and he had made it to Clifton. He had tied up to the dock there and left the motor running until he could call me with a new time to pick them up.

We positively tore back to Frankfort and were there in time to see Jack and little Peter coming safely into the dock. I was never so glad to see anybody in my life.

Coming back to Midway after a thirty-minute hassle that was our usual experience in getting the boat out of the water and on to that stupid trailer. I heard Jenny talking to Matt—they had made the second wild dash to Frankfort with Ann T and me because they did not want to miss out on any of the drama. She said, "This has been the longest and worst day of my life." Amen.

NOVEMBER 6TH

Sunday night, we went to Ben and Ruth's and chatted about taking Jim Gay into the office as a partner. Ben told us about the home visit that he made on Mrs. Davis when he was in the old office and she lived just across the street. She spent a lot of her time sitting at her front window, watching people going in and out of that office. Whenever anyone she knew would go in, she would call up wanting to know what was wrong with them.

On this particular day, Mrs. Davis was very sick to her stomach and had called Ben to come. Using his best bedside manner, Ben had gone where she was lying, and he sat on the bed beside her. Just at that moment the bed had given away beneath them, and they both had crashed to the floor in the middle of the covers, mattresses, and a huge pot that Mrs. Davis had kept by her side to be sick in. It was not a home visit that you would be likely to forget.

NOVEMBER 27TH

They were supposed to start framing up the house, but it poured rain all day. I went to the annual Thanksgiving Market Luncheon today at the Christian Church, and it was delicious as always. We went with Mr. Tom, and I ate the usual oyster stew and chicken salad. Through the grace of God, I managed to skip the homemade pies.

DECEMBER 9TH

When Ann T woke up, we went to Taylor Manor to take a little book to Miss Mayme, who was ninety-two today. She was on the sunporch enjoying a church service by Bert Eyster, Singing out on "Faith of Our Fathers." She was the organist at the Baptist Church in Midway for years until she announced to the church one morning that it was her last Sunday—that it was time for someone younger to take over. As I have said before, a most remarkable lady.

DECEMBER 13TH

Jack has caught the flu and feels horrible. Said his skin ached. He has a high fever and a cough. There is a real epidemic going around, and it is driving him crazy that he is unable to help Ben today.

DECEMBER 15TH

Jack went to work yesterday morning and came in at two-thirty desperately sick. His temp was up past 102, his cough was worse, and his chest was sore and raspy. I absolutely panicked remembering the young soldier patient of theirs who died when his flu turned into pneumonia back in 1961. Ben was horribly busy because of the epidemic but managed to come around midnight daily and reassured me that he heard no rattle.

DECEMBER 20TH

Jack stayed home—in bed—with the flu until Wednesday. His chest x-ray remained clear, but I was terribly anxious as this was the first time since he started his practice that he was simply down and out. Thursday night he went to the hospital to do a history and physical on a patient before surgery, but Dr. Crutcher called in with the flu, unable to do the operating, so Jack came on home.

Friday, I went to pick up the Christmas tree the children and I had selected last Monday. This is the first year that we haven't gone with Ben in the big truck to cut a cedar in the field, but Jack just should not get that cold and damp. Ruth and Ben were supposed to go to a really fancy party, but she is down with the flu. I keep expecting to get it—am keeping food stocked up in case.

DECEMBER 26TH

Jack decided to work today even though it is his day off and he still feels like the 'wrath of God'. The student is down with the flu and Ben is still going although he is running a low-grade fever and has a cough. What a motley crew.

DECEMBER 31ST

Jack had a wild night last night making seven house calls even though his cough is back and he looks terrible. He is so tense and tired, but so many people really do need help. We decided to skip the annual Midway New Year's Eve party as Jack was exhausted. I don't believe I can stay awake until midnight, but I hope I can make it until he comes in. Old 1968 is really limping to a close for us.

68

1969

Take it back. It won't do.

—Ben Chandler

JANUARY 12TH

Wednesday night there was a special meeting of the City Council to vote on the annexation of the subdivision that will be behind us when we move. It barely passed.

JANUARY 19TH

My Daddy is dead. I don't know how to write all the events of the past week, but I want to put them down while they are reasonably clear.

Last Monday at noon the phone rang, and it was Mama's nextdoor neighbor saying that Daddy had had a heart attack and for me to come. I called Jack at the office and asked him to call the hospital in Louisville where they had taken my dad, and I would find a baby sitter. I was still on the phone when I saw Jack coming towards the kitchen door, and I knew by the agonized look on his face that Daddy was dead. All the years—all the memories of how kind he was to us—how loving and caring—of what a good Christian man he was—of his guidance—came flooding over me and it was just almost too much to accept the fact that he was gone.

My sister and her husband came immediately from Florida where Jim was on a business trip and together, we managed to get through the next few days. We buried Daddy on Wednesday in Lyon County, the place he always referred to as home, alongside his ancestors, his sister, and his father. He had always loved Lyon County and once told me of the day when he was twelve years old, he went out behind a big tree in the yard and prayed that God would end the world before any one of the family would leave home, as he didn't think he could bear to be separated from them. He has always been a driving force in my life, and I felt an unrelenting loss when I realized that force was gone.

The rest of the week really isn't clear—I did the laundry, cleaned, and our friends came by. Midway is a wonderful place in a time of sadness. Mama seems to be doing fairly well, considering.

JANUARY 25TH

Tonight, a man stabbed his girlfriend in front of her three children here in town. This is the first murder since we have been here. The police have him in custody.

JANUARY 27TH

We are relaxing a couple of days at Shakertown. The oven here is broken, so they gave us a sandwich and coffee. James

Cogar (Jim) came by and took us walking through the fields, meadows, along the bluffs of the river and down around the river bottom. He went at such a fast pace that I had to run to keep up. It was bitter cold, but we were sweating we had gone so fast.

FEBRUARY 7TH

Jimmy Stone walked over to the house to ask how high to put the chair rails and I had not the faintest notion. I hurriedly called Joe Lehman and off the top of his head he said there should be thirty-two inches from the floor to the top of the chair rail. It's nice to have expert friends.

MARCH 1ST

We went with Ben and Ruth to take the student and his wife to Levas' for dinner as this was the end of his stay at the office. The four of us gave him a Julep Cup—he has really been helpful to them.

MARCH 22ND

We went to the Woodford County Hospital's dedication of the new surgical ward at two, and it was nice. Jack was called away on an emergency, so I sat through the entire thing alone—also the tea. The whole day was a little embarrassing, as I don't know those people well. I bummed a ride home with a teacher from the Girls School.

MARCH 30TH

We took Bruce and Patsy Davis to Shakertown to show them the restoration and when we went to dinner, they said Jack was wanted on the phone. It was a doctor in Lexington saying an ambulance had brought William Lehman in, unconscious from an apparent stroke. We went directly to St. Joseph's—we both felt horrible that Jack wasn't there when they needed him. Don't know where Ben was—the office simply must start a call schedule.

APRIL 1ST

The painter came at nine, so I called Joe Lehman and set up a ten-thirty appointment for Miss Elizabeth to help him choose our paint colors. In one hour we had completely chosen all the paint for the whole house, and Joe had found a chair rail that we love. He has been our "Professor Higgins" throughout.

We were delighted to hear that William is recovering nicely.

JUNE 18TH

Today was moving day! And it started at five-thirty a.m. We had already taken everything we possibly could to the new house across the street, so we all sat on the floor to eat breakfast. The children thought this was "neat."

JUNE 23RD

Our thirteenth anniversary and Jack remembered! At five o'clock he called and asked me to get a sitter so we could go out to dinner. I was delighted—I had given up on thinking about it. We went to Levas' and came home early to listen to the record of "Man of La Mancha" which I had given him to commemorate the occasion. Wonderful life for thirteen years.

JULY 21ST

Saturday, we thought we had been invited to the Buster's for a picnic, and Dick and Hilda Starks were to come to pick us up at seven fifteen. As we went out to get in their car, we looked across the street and here came hordes of friends carrying food, drinks, ice, gifts—everything to give us a housewarming! They completely surprised us! Fifty-two people came and every one of them brought a small gift for the house. It was absolutely great. The last people left at one-fifteen a.m., after all the food had been put away and the dishes done. Dick Starks even ran the sweeper.

AUGUST 10TH

Friday night we went to Ben and Toss's for dinner with Bert and Beverly Eyster (Bert is the Presbyterian Minister). Toss had not fixed dinner for company in such a long time that we absolutely badgered her until she set a date. We decided to tease her by dressing formally (Jack borrowed Ben Roach's tux and the shirt was blue with big ruffles down the front. Jack almost died when he saw it.), and by arriving in the Eyster's old 1964 Cadillac sedan, even though they live just a couple of doors up the street from the Chandler's house in Versailles, we could barely keep a straight face as we rang the bell. When the door opened, we were astonished to see Ben and Toss also in formal attire just as surprised at seeing us all dressed up, as if we were all celebrating a real occasion. Not one of us missed a beat. We were ushered in with great dignity and we discussed only world affairs and philosophy. We were then served dinner by the girl who helps them, and she managed not to giggle when serving the wine for Ben to "taste." Ben said with a straight face, "Take it back. It won't do." She took the wine to the kitchen and brought it right back for Ben to accept it as being "fine."

She served curried lamb, salad, and a flaming cherry dessert. All too much—it was wonderful. The fact that it was an incredibly unusual dinner was never mentioned and they saw us out to the huge old musty Cadillac. The next morning, I called Toss at the crack of dawn, and we both laughed until we cried without speaking a word.

AUGUST 20TH

Last Saturday, Jack came in at eleven-thirty wanting to go to the river and get away for a while. We took Pat Clark, and Peter and headed out. Down around three bends in the river from Clifton, there is spot that has a flat sandy bank of about twenty feet, and it is the best spot for relaxing in our entire river area. We had been on this bank about five minutes when the owner of the dock came tearing out in his little run-about, arms waving frantically, calling out that the hospital needed Jack to come now to deliver a baby. We picked up all of our paraphernalia and went with him because I didn't want to risk being stranded on a river on a small strand with two boys as I didn't even know how to swim in case of trouble. Luckily the OB cooperated, and we were back on the river at three. I had to leave at four to get the sitter home, so I picked up Ann T and went to the grocery and was back at the river to get Jack and the boys by six. A frustrating day of trying to relax.

AUGUST 21ST

Matt came home from camp—we had really missed him. He brought us a turtle ash tray and a huge plaque that says,

"God Bless Our Home" in brilliant green and yellow colors, with pink roses on the side. I was in for quite a shock when I opened his suitcase and not one thing had been disturbed from the way I had packed it. The clothes were still clean, and the toothbrush was obviously untouched. He had had a great time.

AUGUST 31ST

Thursday, Newell Hicks came in saying Lucy Bethel, his aunt, had fallen twice in the yard and needed to be hospitalized. He was embarrassed because Ben is out of town, and she has been furious with Jack ever since last year because he did not try to force her to have surgery when he found her cancer. She should have known that it is not Jack's style of practicing medicine. He always believed that the ultimate decision must be left to the patient, after all the options have been explained and discussed. Anyway, she told Newell that she would not let Jack check her, and my understanding husband told Newell that he would admit her to the hospital in Ben's name and she could wait for Ben to come back from vacation before she was examined. Sounds like she is in a bad way.

A lady down the street called in the middle of the night last night, saying that her son had gone crazy, locking himself in the bathroom with a loaded gun, saying he would kill anyone who tried to come in. He was planning on committing suicide. The mother wanted Jack to come down, talk him out of the bathroom, and give him a shot to calm him down. To my utter horror, "Good Old Jack" went—and was able to do exactly what she asked of him. I was pacing the floor until he came back safely.

SEPTEMBER 1ST

Today Jack sowed some grass seed over the yard. The sower was broken in the open position, and he had to run ninety miles an hour, wildly cranking the handle with seed flying all around him over the entire area. He had this awful look on his face, I guess the seeds were flying in his mouth, and eyes as he zoomed around.

OCTOBER 26TH

Lucy Bethel passed away while we were on vacation, and we did not know about it until we came home, it was incredibly sad.

NOVEMBER 25TH

Earlier this month, old Alex Alexander, a pediatrician in Lexington, died while he was asleep in his own bed at the home place, here in Woodford County. His family has owned that farm since the time of Benjamin Franklin. His son, young Alex, came home from Vietnam for the funeral, and Ben approached him about coming into the practice. He agreed to think it over, but was returning to Vietnam to finish his stint.

1970

Are you just a G.P.?
                              —Martha Jane Hutcherson

JANUARY 1ST

Last night Jack and I hosted the annual New Year's Eve party. Fifty-two were invited—the same people that gave us the housewarming—and fifty came. The last couple to leave went out at three in the morning. Jack had to leave to go to the hospital to sew up some accident victims, so I decided to pick up the house while I waited for him. He came in at five-forty-five, and I had the house spotless. We were able to get a couple hours of sleep before I had to go to Louisville to pick up the four children who were staying with Mama.

JANUARY 11TH

The weather has been severe all week. Wednesday the temperature hovered at zero all day. Thursday it went up to five degrees. Friday, eight degrees, Saturday, finally to eighteen. Up to four inches of snow lay on the ground and the children were home from school all week.

FEBRUARY 9TH

On February twenty-eighth and March first, Jack is going to take a test to see if he can become a specialist in Family Practice and I am amazed that he is becoming fairly nervous about it. Sure hope he passes—he is putting his head on the block to try it as it is not required. In the county only Ben and George Reed are trying it with Jack.

MARCH 31ST

John Halpin, a boy who studied under Ben and Jack from the University Med School, has agreed to come into the practice as of July first! He will be here on salary for one year, and if all goes well, he will be on the percentage after that until he works up to being a full partner. He was number one in his class and a real hard worker when he took his rotation at the office. He is down to earth and has a wonderful sense of humor. He is married (Margaret) with two very small children. He is asking for twenty thousand the first year.

When Jack came in tonight, Peter greeted him with, "Hi Dad! Did you know tomorrow is Saint Fool's Day?" Too many saints in a Catholic kindergarten for a five-year-old mind.

Matt had to write, "I will not waste my time at school" two hundred times last night, and he was spelling it "waist" until I saw it and stopped him on number twenty-two. He says he was innocent, but I doubt it.

Jack went to study a course the week of February fifteenth to prepare for the family practice tests. This course was given at the Ramada Inn on Waller just across the street from St. Joseph Hospital in Lexington. One night the roads were slick with rain freezing by the time it hit the ground. When the class was over, Jack was clearing off his windshield from the ice while his motor was running, when he noticed George Reed about three cars down doing the same thing. Jack then got in his car and turned on the defroster and was waiting for the windows to clear. He started to wave to George, but he could not see him, either in the car or scraping the windows. Fearing there was something wrong, Jack got back out to see if he could be of some help. To his disbelief he found George lying on the ground between his car and the next, in all the ice and snow, passed out, not breathing, and with no heart beat that Jack could find.

There was another doctor in the parking lot who was just coming out from the course, and there were some firemen who had been called there for a false alarm, and they all came running when Jack gave a shout. Through all their efforts, they finally managed to get George's heart going—irregularly but going—until a stretcher could be brought from across the street.

Jack called Nell (George's wife) and told her to come but to come carefully because of the roads, and he would wait there until she arrived from Versailles. After she came, he talked to her until she was calm, and then he went back to the parking lot to start home once again. There in the lot, with the motor still running as it had been, for the last hour and a half, was George's beautiful black Lincoln Continental. I guess there were no car thieves out on Waller Avenue on such a terrible night.

APRIL 2ND

Jack went to the hospital tonight to catch up on his charts and ran into two other doctors there. The hospital is to be inspected a week from today and all charts have to be caught up for it to stay accredited.

APRIL 6TH

Nat Parrish is dead, and we are all the lesser for it. I want to take a few minutes this morning to write about her because she has been such a major influence in Midway for so many years.

She was born with a hare lip and a cleft palate that was noticeable for about five minutes after you met her. Then her wonderful wit and warmth took over and you couldn't possibly imagine that she had a handicap. She was "Aunt Des's" daughter and she never married. She lived out her life in the big old house on the hill just as you turn off US 421 towards Midway. She was active in all affairs of the town and was the organist for the Presbyterian Church and the backbone of the Woman's Club, but the thing I remember about her most was her tremendous enthusiasm, her zest for life. Whenever a new couple moved to town, Nat was the first to welcome them and to introduce them to her friends, which, of course, was all of Midway. I never knew her to say a bad word about another soul, she loved the whole human race.

There are so many wonderful stories about Nat, and I'll take time to jot down a couple because I don't want them to be forgotten.

Once when she was the organist for the church, she overslept one Sunday, so she slipped her fur coat over her gown and ran quickly down to play. Another Sunday she was bored with the same old church music every week, so she played, "Yes, We Have No Bananas" very slowly and with a solemn look on her face and not a single person recognized the melody.

A state trooper caught her speeding when she went twenty miles from home and was caught without her license. She begged him to let her go get it, promising faithfully to be back in ten minutes.

I wrote a poem to put on all my Christmas cards one year and the following year she had written a far better verse than me:

> *May Heaven send good will to men,*
> *And help us every one*
> *To keep the Christmas spirit*
> *When the day itself is done.*

Nat managed to keep the Christmas spirit every single day of her life. She was one person that was able to make a difference in the lives of people that she met.

APRIL 10TH

Jack and Ben are officially Family Practitioners as they both passed their tests! They are no longer "justa G.P." even though I was never sure just how funny Jack thinks it is. I remember years ago when some friends of mine from Louisville moved to this area, and I invited them over to meet Jack and some friends. When I introduced them to Jack, Martha Jane Hutcherson looked up at him with a big smile on her face and said, "Are you just a G.P.?"

We teased her about it for years—she went on to become one of Jack's most loyal patients and best friends and he called her "Justa" for a long, long time.

JUNE 24TH

The children of the neighborhood planned a surprise birthday party for Jack. Sixteen of them, including Jenny and Matt, arrived early, and iced down cokes in our basement. They decorated the big room down there with crepe paper, balloons, and signs. They put the entire thirty-eight candles on the cake, lit them too soon and they melted down in the icing. The children had collected money from each child and bought Jack an expensive, horrendously loud, and wide necktie, which he simply MUST wear for them! The party was a huge success, and he was very touched by their thoughtfulness. They played games and ping-pong with him until I chased them out at ten-o-clock.

JULY 23RD

John Halpin has been in the office two weeks, and he is going great guns. Margaret is only twenty-two years old, and makes me feel ancient. John is relieving them of so many drop-ins that he is worth his weight in gold.

SEPTEMBER 14TH

Last week I went to visit Miss Mayme Cogar at Taylor Manor and she told me some interesting things about old Midway. She said that during the Civil War, four Confederate soldiers were taken behind the Presbyterian Church and shot "in retaliation." All the townspeople went into their homes and pulled the shades. It was the blackest day in the History of Midway. Years later, Mrs. Margaret Foster's mother raised the money to have their bodies moved to the cemetery and now a big stone marks their grave. When Miss Mayme was a child, she and her friends would tell other children, "Go and sit on the Confederates' tombstones and ask them what they were shot for. And, if you listen closely, you will hear them answer, 'nothing at all'."

She told me that her parent's house was the first one on Winter Street and she had watched every other house being built when she was a child. She saw them move Jim Raisor's house in two pieces from Mrs. William Wise's corner, where it had been a schoolhouse, to its present site one block away. She said when Mr. Tom married Mrs. Roach, they first lived in an apartment in Midway, then they moved to the farm, where Ben was born. They still call that "The Home Place". Then they bought the house on Winter Street.

Miss Mayme went on to tell about the big festivities in 1933 when Midway celebrated its first one hundred years. The celebration was held at the Girls School, and everyone dressed in costume. The railroad built a platform for the school and there was much activity. All the stores had special displays in their windows—one of them borrowed the silver from the Cannons that had been on the Robert E. Lee Steamboat. Miss Mayme will be ninety-four in December—I hope all the talking didn't tire her out too much.

DECEMBER 18TH

We are giving Jenny art supplies and a tiny transistor radio for Christmas. Matt is getting a new bicycle and nothing else. Peter, a child's record player with three records, and Ann T a rocking chair and a doll. Jack and I are going light for each other because of the constant lack of funds—I am giving him a Parker ball point pen but I have ordered two volumes of Sandburg's Lincoln for him from Mama's Christmas money.

DECEMBER 21ST

John is still working hard in the practice, but I'm not as sure as I was that he will be happy here. He seems to want a different kind of practice than the one Ben and Jack have established. It is almost as if he wants just an eight to five day with no night calls and no home visits except in dire emergencies. Jack and Ben don't want to practice like that, and I'm not sure the patients would stand for it anyhow. John gets upset when a patient comes knocking on his door even when he is on call (he has set up a call-schedule and that has been a Godsend for Jack) to say nothing of when he is not on call.

The other night a patient banged at his door after midnight and John fussed at him for not phoning first, but then took care of the man. Just as he got back to bed, there was another knock at the door, and he was pretty mad when he answered it. It was the same man and John started to let him have it. The man interrupted him, saying, "I'm sorry to bother you again, Dr. Halpin, but I just saw your baby boy running down the street in his pajamas. I thought you should know." John felt chagrined as he went tearing down the street in search of Baby Halpin, who had almost reached the corner by this time.

John is one of my favorite people—I do hope it can all be worked out.

1971

Come on out Doc. I know you're in there.

—Determined Patient

JANUARY 17TH

I talked to my sister Ann and her husband Jim three times today trying to make arrangements for his mother, Belinda Bowling (Bo) to go into Taylor Manor. They have a room she could have at three hundred twenty-five dollars in the new wing where she could have a great deal of privacy. Ann and Jim are coming from Connecticut on Saturday to meet with the main Sister and to look at the room. Bo has gotten quite senile, and I am sure the move will be hard on her.

JANUARY 24TH

Last night at the hospital, Jack went in to check a cantankerous old lady who was angry at him to start with. She was facing the wall with her back to him and gave no indication that she knew he had come into her room. He said something to her and put his finger on her wrist to take her pulse. Just then a glorious baritone voice came over the intercom singing "The Lord's Prayer".

Jack respectfully waited until the song was finished, before he resumed the examination. Just as the last note ended the lady spoke up without looking around, in a clearly disgruntled voice, "Singin' to me ain't goin' to make any difference, Dr. Fisher. I'm still mad at you."

Considering that Jack has a voice only a mother could love, it was hard for him to keep a straight face while he finished the exam.

FEBRUARY 13TH

Bo is now at Taylor Manor and seems content. She is far more senile than I realized—desperately wanting an apartment, which is out of the question now. She likes the ladies there and the routine, but she wants a "project." I have been dashing in and out every other day for just a few minutes and am convinced that she is past the time for "projects." How utterly sad for such a brilliant mind.

FEBRUARY 15TH

Bo was here for the afternoon yesterday and seemed pleased about going back. I think things are working out. Her best friend at Taylor Manor is Mrs. Epstein, a little Jewish lady from Midway who is senile to the point of thinking she is Jesus Christ.

Her people were Russian immigrants who came to Midway and opened a dry goods store years ago. She and her sister were both very short, and used to drive an old Oldsmobile that they maneuvered by looking out through the steering wheel to see where they were going. All four fenders were rounded off where they had had accidents and they told Jack that whenever they met a car, they would close their eyes and just hope they got by alright.

Jack persuaded them both to go to Taylor Manor after he had made several home visits and found the gas on the kitchen stove left partially on. The sister died a few years back, and now this lady pushes Bo around all day in a wheelchair and it makes them both happy.

Jim (Bowling) has a Jewish friend in Washington, D.C. who is terribly bright and funny, even to the point of being a speech writer for one of the leading politicians in the country. Jim called his friend the other day and said, "I think I have a story you can't top. I have a Baptist mother who is living in a Catholic nursing home, whose best friend there is a Jewish lady who thinks she is Jesus Christ."

For the first time in his life, the speech writer was speechless.

MARCH 15TH

Ben and Toss had supper with us last night and we got to laughing about the time Whit was a baby and came down with the croup. He was wheezing and coughing, and they called Jack about three a.m. because they were scared.

He went right over and as they did not have a vaporizer, he told them to take the baby into their bathroom, close the door, and to run the hot water to try to create enough steam to relieve the congestion.

Jack gave Whit a shot to help, and then the four of them crowded into the small bathroom in the old house they had renovated. The bathtub set high on funny little legs and Ben turned on the hot water spigot. A small thread of water trickled out and Jack told him to turn it on full blast. Ben looked up wild-eyed and said, "That's as full as she'll go!!"

It was obvious that they were in for a long night so Jack told Ben to go make a pot of coffee and they would wait out the congestion. The three of them sat in that tiny bathroom hovering over the baby, drinking coffee, and talking until little Whit finally fell asleep—probably from sheer exhaustion.

APRIL 7TH

I took Bo Bowling to Dr. Jim Pope last Thursday to have her eyes tested, and there were five other patients waiting in the reception room, staring into space the way people do who are waiting to see a doctor. She said in a loud voice, "Look, isn't it curious that he has put all these manikins out here in these chairs! Why do you think he has done that?"

Red-faced, I kept trying to tell her that these people were just waiting like we were, whereupon she said loudly, "Isn't it curious that they don't move." Finally, I managed to get the subject changed and we were chatting away about every day things when she motioned to a fat lady who was sitting just across the aisle from us. The lady had on a brilliant red suit that was very short and very tight. I held my breath as Bo began loudly, "I used to have a suit like that. My skirt wasn't that short, and it didn't fit that tight, but it was exactly that color."

The lady in red sat bold up-right and I jumped up from the chair to ask to be put in an examining room right away, regardless of when we were seen. The nurse, who had witnessed the entire episode, came to the rescue and we were ushered back immediately.

A little later Dr. Pope came in, examined her eyes, and gave us a good report. I had wanted to take her to him because he reminded me so much of her son Jim, and I thought she would like him. He had been a general practitioner for a few years in Eastern Kentucky, but he did not enjoy the hours. He told us about the night a patient came knocking at his door around two a.m. As he was exhausted, he decided to ignore the screen at the open window by his bed, and he heard a quiet voice say, "Come on out, Doc, I know you're in there."

He applied for a residency the next day.

AUGUST 30TH

Jack has gone to the office with Ben, John and lawyer friend, Joe Arnold, to legally draw up the partnership papers. John will draw twenty-five percent this year and Ben and Jack will each draw thirty-seven and one-half percent. Each year John's proportion will increase slightly until 1975, when each will draw thirty-three and one third percent.

OCTOBER 15TH

Sunday night we were staying at Beaumont Inn and had just gone to bed when the phone rang. It was Catherine Hicks, Niesje's daughter, in labor and she wanted Jack to come to the Woodford Hospital to deliver her. I decided to ride over with him as it was so very late. We arrived at one-thirty and the baby came at five-thirty. Another of Jack's OBs had come in around four, so we stayed until she delivered at eight-thirty in the morning. I had read an entire little book while I waited, and I was glad to be there to drive Jack back to Beaumont where they had a fantastic breakfast waiting for us.

OCTOBER 18TH

Last Thursday evening Ben called us to come up for a minute. Alex Alexander had stopped by his house and said that after much consideration, he did want to come into the practice, if he was still wanted. Ben said indeed he was wanted, and they discussed salary and percentages. Ben then called Jack to make sure he still wanted Alex, and Jack said he definitely did. When John was asked, he said he was willing to call the advisors in Louisville and abide by their opinion, so I guess he did not understand that Ben and Jack definitely want Alex and have already negotiated with him. A problem.

NOVEMBER 2ND

Election Day and the last time Jack will run for City Council for a while. He has been getting the most votes of any of the other candidates and Ike Rouse says that happens every time because more people owe Jack money than any of the others. Hmmm.

1972

I'd call that a hinkey.

—Dr. Alex Alexander

JANUARY 19TH

Ben and Jack finally talked to John—told him that the partnership isn't working out. He was surprised to hear this and said he would look into a residency starting July first. He will be in the practice until then. They are both very fond of John. It is always sad when a relationship with people you really care about simply does not work out.

FEBRUARY 3RD

Snow has covered the ground this morning and more is falling. Because of the strong winds there are deep drifts everywhere. Winter snows in Midway always remind me of the storm we had on one Saturday back in 1961. Along with Ben and Ruth, and Jim and Sarah Raisor, we were invited to Dick and Hilda Starks for a steak dinner and had made up our minds that we were going no matter what.

All day long the snow fell, and the wind whistled, building up huge drifts on the Midway–Versailles Road where the Starks lived, about three miles from town.

The six of us piled into Jack's big old four door Oldsmobile that had belonged to Mr. Fisher, and we started out. Just outside of Midway, we were headed up a hill with enormous snowbanks on either side when the car began to slide. Ben yelled, "Hit it Norm!"

Jack hit the accelerator and the car spun all around and nose-dived into a snow drift that was about four feet high. We all climbed out of the left side doors of the car and saw that the car was there for the duration. Ben stated, "We're almost there now, we might as well go on out." This was not true as we were still in sight of the town, but no one questioned this obviously erroneous judgement, and we began trudging through the snow in the direction of the Starkses. The wind was blowing snow in our eyes so that we could hardly see. It was like a blizzard.

At Nugent's Cross Roads, when we really were about half-way there, Sarah gave out. She said she simply could go no farther. Jack and Ben thought she was experiencing some angina, but we couldn't stop here—we had to go on. The two of them got on either side of her and literally carried her on down the road.

The drifts had grown so deep that walking in the road became impossible. We climbed the fence lifting Sarah bodily over, and walked the fields staying close enough to the road to tell where we were. At least three more fences were crossed before we saw the porch light at the Starks house. No beacon light in the world had ever been more welcome. My leg was bleeding—I had no idea why—and Sarah's skirt was torn. Other than that, we were almost nonetheless for wear.

We ate a good steak dinner and played a round or two of bridge in front of a blazing fire, and then we knew we had to come home. Jim and Sarah decided to stay the night, but the other hearty souls struck out once again across the fields. By now the snow had stopped falling, the wind was still, the moon had come out, and the world was incredibly beautiful. With the moonlight on the snow, it was as bright as day and was easy to make our way. We eased ourselves into our beds at home around two a.m.

Jim and Sarah walked to town the next afternoon accompanied by Dick and Hilda as the roads were still closed to traffic and the Starkses worried that Sarah might need assistance again. Jim had a bad night. He and Sarah were sleeping in the big old bed that belonged to the Starks' daughter and the old Collie dog slept under the bed. During the night, Jim needed to go to the bathroom, but every time he would swing his leg over the side, the dog would give a low, menacing growl and Jim would hastily withdraw the leg. He barely managed to survive until morning.

It was such great fun and I never see a snow–drifted Midway Road but what I think of that memorable night.

APRIL 12TH

Barbara Grimes, the receptionist at the office is a little hard of hearing in one ear. Last week she glanced out of the desk window at a man who had just come in and she wanted to get out his medical chart, but she could not remember his name. She asked Ann Lewis (another girl working in the office) who he was, and she looked out and said, "Offhand I don't know."

"Of course," replied Barbara, "How could I forget Orville Hannah."

JUNE 24TH

John and Margaret Halpin are gone. The movers came Wednesday, and they headed out for the Mayo Clinic, bag and baggage. I hope they will remember us kindly.

JULY 7TH

Saw an Indigo Bunting this morning—great way to start any day.

JULY 11TH

Jack, Ben, and Alex are meeting at five-thirty to make the necessary decisions about coming in with them. Afterwards, we are all having dinner at Ben and Ruth's.

JULY 12TH

Today I picked up Alex's sign to go on the office door and had the old Caduceus shined up. Jack and Ben met with him last night and offered him twenty thousand a year. Jack and I are very fond of him—hope the bubble doesn't burst.

JULY 14TH

I was wondering out loud to Jack tonight if the time would ever come when we would not have to fret over the children. He says it will never happen. That a few years back he went to see old Mary Anderson who was ninety-six at the time and whose two children (aged seventy-one and seventy-three) were back home living with her. They both enjoyed a drink every now and then and liked to smoke in bed, so Jack was worried that she might come to harm living there. It was a worrisome situation and Jack was trying to persuade her to go to Taylor Manor.

"I can't go, Dr. Fisher," she declared, "I'd worry too much about the children."

We came to the conclusion that it never ends—worrying about "the children" is a life-long curse to bear.

SEPTEMBER 10TH

Ann T went to school today, and I am despondent over losing my last child. One phase of my life is probably over. She was great fun for me to have here at home and I miss her.

OCTOBER 7TH

Jack worked two hours last night to get a nosebleed to stop. He vows that when he dies, if he goes to Hell, he will be forced to treat nose bleeds for an eternity. As far as he is concerned, that is the most frustrating area of general practice. For Alex, it is delivering babies.

OCTOBER 30TH

Alex sent a bottle of wine over tonight with a note of how much you need it on the first day back from vacation. He had a pretty rough time while Jack was gone.

NOVEMBER 24TH

This past Monday night, Mrs. Bowling went to sleep at Taylor Manor and died. I had to call my brother-in-law because Jack was in a delivery, and it was the hardest thing I have ever had to do. Poor old Bo. Her life had become so undignified.

The boom was lowered last weekend when Alex told Jack that he didn't want to stay in the practice. He said he would stay until they could find someone else, but he did not want to spend the rest of his life doing this kind of work. We are heartsick, but this is not the kind of job anyone can do if their heart isn't in it. We want him to be happy above all else.

DECEMBER 2ND

Jack had to make a home visit on an elderly lady that he is called for fairly often. When he went to check her, he realized she still had on all her clothes—even her shoes. He surmises that she had been up all day and jumped in bed when she saw him coming up the walk. Her husband carves the wonderful chains from one piece of wood, and he gave one to Jack.

DECEMBER 10TH

Last week a lady was waiting in the hall at the office to catch Alex when he came out of an examining room. When he appeared, she pulled at his sleeve and leaned her face towards his, pointing with her finger to a place on her forehead.

"Dr. Alexander," she called nervously. "Just what would you call this?"

Alex peered down at her through his giant horn-rimmed glasses and answered, "I'd call that a hinkey," and went on down the hall.

1973

MARCH 22ND

Jack had a checkup with an Internist today and everything is A-OK. As Jack's resting heartbeat is sort of high, the Doc suggested that he start some sort of regular exercise. Jack is going back to see him for a checkup every other year.

APRIL 9TH

The past week wasn't too exciting. Alex is gone from the office on vacation, so Jack is on call every other night. He also delivered six babies in the last seven days so he was not here very often.

MAY 7TH

Jack has started jogging back over the hill in the new subdivision every night. He runs at night after all of his calls even though he is usually exhausted, because he is so embarrassed to be running at all, and he hopes no one will see him up there after dark.

JULY 11TH

I took Mrs. Roach to Lehman's today and accidently closed the car door on her hand. We rushed in the shop to get an icepack on it. She was very nice to me, but I have been heartsick about it all day. Her mental cycle has been very high lately, and when one of the aides from Taylor Manor took her for a ride in Versailles last week, she said, "Stop the car. I want to buy that dress in the shop's window. Please go in and charge it to me."

The aide was hesitant and said, "But Mrs. Roach, you don't know what size it is. Who were you planning to give it to?"

"I'll give it to the one it fits," Mrs. Roach explained logically, and the aide could not dissuade her. They purchased the dress.

AUGUST 14TH

Jack is at the hospital—he is assisting with a D&C on a patient having a miscarriage. Mildred Buster called a minute ago saying that Bill had almost cut off the end of his finger. Considering the fact that he has just one arm this was doubly serious. I told her to bring him to the office and I would round up Jack. I called the hospital for him, but he could not leave his OB. He said for me to meet the Busters at the office and to direct them on to the hospital and he would treat Bill's finger there.

I ran out to the garage in a hurry so I would be at the office when they arrived. And there was no car in the garage! Jenny had taken it to go to church! So, I tore out on Matt's bicycle and managed not to have a wreck on it. I was waiting there when they drove up and I sent them on.

AUGUST 18TH

Wanted to have a fancy dinner tonight for Jim Cogar and Jim Thomas and his wife. The hospital called telling me that Jack had an OB in and I went into a tailspin. I didn't feel like I could ask Jim T. to make the drinks, cook the steaks, and do everything! I was reminded of the story that Jim C. tells about his mother going to the Opera in Midway in the old golden days when there was an Opera House up above where the drugstore is today. Her driver, a man named William, was a person who liked to imbibe when the occasion arose. While Mrs. Cogar was in the Opera, he waited for her at the buggy and tasted a few. By the time she came out, he was feeling no pain. Going home out the Midway/Versailles Road, he drove the buggy right past the gate to the house.

"William!" called out Mrs. Cogar. "You have passed the gate!"

He answered, "Mrs. Cogar, I can't drive the buggy and carry the whip and do everything."

Anyway, Jim T. missed cooking the steaks, making the drinks, and doing everything, because Jack came roaring in just in time. He had to rush back to the hospital after eating one bite of meat but was home again before the evening was over.

AUGUST 22ND

There will soon be an exit off the new interstate just one mile from Midway and we dread the repercussions. There is a rumor going around that the Holiday Inn is interested in opening a motel at the interchange, and that some landowners have been negotiating with them. The town is up in arms, and there is much talk about circulating petitions to stop it.

AUGUST 25TH

I signed a petition today to try to raise the limit per house on land zoned for agriculture to fifteen acres up from the present requirement of five. A man from Lexington is proposing an elaborate subdivision on the beautiful historic Old Frankfort Pike and most of us just don't want it to happen.

AUGUST 25TH

We have formed a group called "Woodford Save the Land" and it is headed up by Libby Jones. She presented our request for the acreage change and they voted unanimously in our favor. We have won the first battle. Now on to the Public Hearing of the Zoning Board where the Lexington man will present his side of the case.

AUGUST 30TH

Today the strip of Interstate opened from Frankfort to Lexington, and I dread the circumstances. We all fear the possibilities of high rises, motels, gas stations and shopping centers at the interchange if we are not on our toes.

SEPTEMBER 1ST

I am incredibly overwhelmingly sad. Alex is not in the practice any more as of today. Yesterday the girls at the office called to see if I would run to Frankfort and pick up a pizza so we could have a party on his last day. I think he was genuinely touched by their thoughtfulness.

LABOR DAY 1973

This morning early the police woke us up by ringing the back door bell. Bill Clark had not seen the car coming on 421 and had crashed into Sarah Hicks and her boyfriend Fred. Fred's ear was bleeding badly but no one else was hurt. I fixed a big pot of coffee, and we were all having a cup when Lily May, Bill's wife, came tearing in to see if anyone was hurt. She joined us for a cup of coffee and our day had officially begun.

SEPTEMBER 4TH

Jack took down Alex's sign from the front of the office and we stuck it in the attic here, not quite ready to let it go.

SEPTEMBER 17TH

The Zoning Board's public hearing regarding the proposed subdivision on the Old Frankfort Pike was held Thursday night and it was wild. There were maybe four hundred people there and I would guess three hundred and ninety-six were on our side. It turned out to be a contest for the lawyers and it lasted until one o'clock in the morning, whereupon it was dismissed until September twenty-seventh. Hopefully some ordinary people will get heard that evening and the lawyers will take a rest.

SEPTEMBER 24TH

On Sunday around eleven p.m., the phone rang, and it was told to Jack that Mrs. Fred (Edna) Wherle was killed in a head-on collision and Mr. Fred was hospitalized in serious condition. It breaks my heart to remember how much she did not want to give up the farm and move. As long as we have been in Midway, she has had a certain irregular heart beat every now and then and she would have to have Ben or Jack come immediately when it started up to give her a shot to slow down the beat. This would not have been so bad except they lived out in the country and did not have a phone. At one time it seemed like every time we were going somewhere, there would be Mr. Fred flagging us down to come quick.

Anyway, the family asked Jack to tell Edna's sister, who lived in Midway and was aged about ninety, before she had the chance to read it in the paper. I don't envy him the task.

SEPTEMBER 25TH

Jack came home yesterday saying it had been a long, wild day. He and Ben are being sued for five hundred and sixteen thousand dollars by a patient they committed to a mental institution. She is also suing her daughter and son because they asked that she be committed. Both Jack and Ben had signed the papers because after checking her thoroughly they had agreed that she was definitely mentally deranged. The headache is back.

OCTOBER 3RD

On Thursday we went to the Zoning Board's second public hearing, and it was much more to my liking. Several people got up and made their views known, and some were quite effective. The meeting was over by eleven-thirty p.m. with the announcement that the Board has forty-five days in which to reach its verdict.

Bob Biddle has just been approached about coming into the Practice and he called to say he is interested. Jack and Ben both liked him so very much when he did his rotation for family practice down here and the patients seemed to take to him. He is coming to talk on Saturday and will be here for good by the end of June, if things work out.

OCTOBER 12TH

Yesterday we went to the final zoning meeting on the proposed subdivision on the Old Frankfort Pike. The Board turned down the request on the grounds that it would need a zone change, and they do not feel that this is warranted. Whew!! The Old Frankfort Pike is just about the most beautiful Pike left in existence in Kentucky. I can't imagine it being changed in any way. It is still two lane, totally shaded by age-old trees, with the great stone walls running for miles and miles on both sides, giving the feeling of ancient durability and lasting beauty. It should never be sacrificed in the name of 'progress'.

OCTOBER 20TH

Tuesday, we paid the boat man in Frankfort thirty dollars to haul Jack's boat out of the water. It was sheer disappointment for him this summer. Every single time we went out, we had trouble.

NOVEMBER 11TH

The zoning study of Midway should be through by April or May they tell us, and we can ponder which way we are going as a community.

NOVEMBER 17TH

Friday, I signed a petition against the extension of the Bluegrass Parkway. Its path would run right through some of the most fertile, historic land in the state. And there is simply no traffic to justify such an extension. There is quite a movement in the county to stop it.

Midway is beginning to change as a result of the interstate exit—I do hope it can hold on to its charm. Several specialty shops have opened, and they are quite an addition to the town.

DECEMBER 10TH

Yesterday, we gave a party to celebrate Miss Mayme Cogar's ninety-seventh birthday. She came at five o'clock p.m. with Jim Cogar, Jim Thomas and his wife and Bill.

We ate at six o-clock, and they took her back to Taylor Manor at seven. We were all just glad she felt like coming.

Jack is at his last City Council meeting as he has decided not to run for re-election. It is almost eleven and he is not home yet, I guess there is a lot to do with all the new stores in town. There are two more shops opening down on Main Street. I hope they can all survive.

DECEMBER 12TH

A red-letter day! Bob Biddle called to say that the terms Jack had written him were acceptable and they would be here as of July first, ready to roll.

Good news and bad news depending how you look at it. The poor lady who was suing Ben and Jack has passed away. I hate to say this, but it is a relief. Of course, the suit is dropped.

DECEMBER 25TH

Ninety-five-year-old Monsignor Hillenmeyer gave Mass this morning at Taylor Manor and he talked about the kind of lives we must attempt to live—lives of justice, of charity and of temperance. Using no notes, he just looked straight at you, and you got the message. His favorite phrase is "and the like and so on" and we have become very partial to it too.

DECEMBER 29TH

Christmas was magic this year with Peter and Ann T miraculously still believing. We all six decorated the tree, and I strung popcorn and cranberries on the lengths of thread. Mama arrived on the two-thirty bus and she was so happy just to be with the children. We all dressed in our best for the Christmas Eve dinner, and Jenny read the scripture from Luke.

Ahead of the Hounds

1974

There is nothing in life that would be harder on my marriage than buckets of money.

—Jack Fisher

JANUARY 1ST

Jack and I stayed home this New Year's Eve for the first time in years and loved it. Jenny sat for a teacher's baby, Peter and Ann T went to bed early, and Matt, Jack and I watched on TV as Notre Dame defeated number one Alabama by a score of twenty-four to twenty-three in a most exciting game. Jack had to go to the office and did not get back by midnight, so Matt and I had a sip of champagne to celebrate, and then took the huge iron triangle out and rang it up and down the street. Missy and Patti Bright shot off some firecrackers and the church bells rang. It was very festive. When Jack came home at one-thirty, we had a glass of champagne to drink to old 1973 and to the hope of 1974.

JANUARY 6TH

The hours at the office have always been full days, five days a week, with Ben taking off on Wednesdays and Jack on Thursdays, and a half day on Saturdays for everyone. The girls alternate afternoons off, and this prevents them from riding together from Versailles where four of them live.

Jack has suggested to Ben that they dispense with Saturday hours and just have a doctor on call to cover all calls. As it is, Jack is never home on Saturdays before three or three-thirty, even though it is called 'a half-day'. He would rather work one hard, long Saturday and get the next one off entirely. He is counting on the staff at the office to talk Ben into this plan, as it would give the girls five straight days of working with every weekend free.

JANUARY 23RD

Jack came in for supper at ten after eight—he didn't finish at the office in time to go to the Civil War Round Table. Lucky for him, I had a premonition and had saved him a pork chop. He had a stack of at least fifty medical charts to write on from the office that he hadn't had time to do today.

JANUARY 27TH

Jack missed Mass today because his OB had a prolapsed cord, but they were able to do a Cesarean in time. Mother and baby are fine. He jogged tonight at ten-thirty and is now doing sit-ups. His physical fitness jag is continuing.

FEBRUARY 21ST

Jack left home at two in the morning to deliver a breech baby. He was unsuccessful and had to call an obstetrician. Needless to say, he was up the rest of the night, coming home at ten a.m.

FEBRUARY 23RD

I had a fight with a patient last night and that always unnerves me. A man called and Jenny answered the phone saying her dad was not on call and would he please call Ben. He shouted at her, cursing, and using vile language. She burst out crying. I dialed the number he had given her and lambasted him. I told him never to talk that way to our daughter again, and indeed, Jack would not be available to him that evening. He yelled at me, but I yelled last—I was furious. I made Jenny promise not to tell Jack about the episode as he would probably want to call the jerk anyway. I tore up his number.

MARCH 11TH

Jenny has the lead in the school production of "Annie Get Your Gun", and she has to come up with seven different costumes for the part. Jack called the lady who first planned to sue the office for her fall there, but changed her mind and became one of Jack's very favorite patients. She had lived in Montana for forty previous years and is lending Jenny two marvelous Western hats and beautiful Indian-made gloves. Great!

MARCH 25TH

We laughed at Jim Cogar last night when we were there for dinner. We were looking through one of his old photograph albums when we came upon a lady we did not know. Jim off-handedly said, "Oh, that's just Marie of Romania." And it actually was! It was made when she visited Williamsburg when he was with the restoration there. Too funny.

APRIL 4TH

April third will long be a day to be remembered in Kentucky as the state was blasted by a tornado. It hit Louisville and headed East toward Frankfort. Jack was called to the hospital as it came towards us and he stayed there most of the night. He learned this morning that two of his patients had died who lived in a mobile home near Frankfort. When they heard the tornado was coming, they lay down on the floor, placing their bodies over their children to protect them, and they were killed when the storm hit. The children escaped without a scratch.

APRIL 6TH

Bob Biddle came to look at housing here and we were delighted that two desirable ones are available. He has lost forty-seven pounds in two months by this amazing diet: black coffee and a hard-boiled egg for breakfast; ham, cheese, cottage cheese and lettuce for lunch; black coffee for supper. Coupled with his strenuous schedule it has really worked for him. It can't possibly be good for a person though. Jack was at a church retreat, so I spent the day with Bob and was delighted to get to know him.

Jenny returned the costumes she had borrowed, and the lady gave her the fancy Indian gloves to keep. Jenny was thrilled—they are perfectly lovely.

APRIL 10TH

Supper was hurried. Jenny was going to an art class downtown, Jack was off to Parish Council and I was going to a meeting to see if we could get the Midway Bicentennial off the ground. We met in the Christian Church, and there were seven of us. We decided to have it in June.

John Willie, our policeman, told me some interesting tales about Midway including the one about the Confederates who were shot 'in retaliation' that Miss Mayme talks about. He added that they had their hands tied behind them and were riding on their coffins in a wagon through town. He said that they went down where the diaper business is now, and had to dig their own graves, then sit on the side of their coffins to be shot in the back so they would fall into them. How perfectly horrible! No wonder the townspeople had pulled down their shades. Not Midway's finest hour to say the least.

MAY 2ND

Yesterday was spent going back and forth to Lexington. Or should I say "forth and back" as Jim Cogar says that's the way it really is.

MAY 19TH

Saturday morning a good lawyer friend from Versailles came by at eight-thirty to talk to Jack about an investment. He wanted us to invest ten thousand dollars and said, "it would mean more money than we ever dreamed of—literally buckets of money." Without batting an eye, Jack answered him, "It is great of you to ask us, but we will have to decline. There is nothing in life that would be harder on my marriage than buckets of money."

Reluctantly I had to agree. I'm not looking for a change in any direction—not even for buckets of money. He was nice to ask us though.

MAY 26TH

It has begun. Yesterday a bus full of tourists rolled into town. Midway people were staring at them as much as they were staring at us. The bus had to drive around for a while to find a place large enough to park.

JUNE 10TH

Tonight, Alex came to see Jack to talk business. He wants to come back into the practice with Ben, Bob and Jack. He said he wanted to live his life and practice his medicine in Woodford County. That the practice wouldn't be as hectic with four and he would enjoy it more. Jack is not sure that the practice is large enough to support four but he agreed to talk to the other two about it.

JUNE 11TH

After a long discussion with Ben and Bob, the decision was reached to take Alex back into the fold.

Every now and then Jack gets a letter from a patient that makes it all seem worthwhile. One such letter came to the office today:

Dear Dr. Fisher,

Thank you so much for being involved in this pregnancy and birth. Your positive attitude made it a much more pleasant experience. When we came to your office the day of the birth, it was so nice to be taken care of by caring hands. Your hands are so healing. That's so rare these days. Do all you must to preserve that valuable quality.

JUNE 12TH

Mr. Tom's birthday and I'm sure he isn't even aware of it. It is the first year I haven't taken a present to him from Ann T since she was born. He doesn't know anybody now and it breaks my heart. He and Mrs. Roach are both at Taylor Manor and I went to see them this afternoon. He did not know I was there.

I walked down the hall to see Miss Mayme Cogar and we had a thirty-minute chat. Her eyes had gone bad on her, and she can't see the printed word anymore. What a catastrophe for Miss Mayme. She was not complaining, but I could see how upset she was.

I remembered the afternoon a couple of years ago when I went to visit her and found her reading "Gone with the Wind" with the enthusiasm of a teenager. Not being able to read will be a real handicap for her. Also last week she had gone to the funeral of the woman who had always promised to take care of Miss Mayme in her old age, and this had upset her as well. It is the first time ever for me to leave Miss Mayme's room anything less than cheerful.

JUNE 17TH

Bob Bibble just called and said he is planning on being in the office on July first. Thus, Jack has just one more Monday of being alone at the office. It has been very hard on him since Ben has been going on Mondays to the University to help set up their family practice unit.

Went to a meeting to see what we could do about the Zoning Midway plan. Only nine people came, and we decided something must be agreed upon before we can get federal aid for our sewers. It is just so vitally important that we get this thing right.

JUNE 18TH

Ben came down to talk to Jack about the office and got to talking about Mr. Tom. He said that his Daddy had always been gentle and kind and these characteristics have stayed with him throughout his illness. He gets very emotional talking about his Dad and I get choked up just listening.

Ben wants Alex to wait a month or two before coming back because of finances and maybe start in September. That way Bob Biddle would have his foot in the door and be earning almost his own way. That makes more sense than both starting on July first.

JUNE 25TH

The lady who gave Jenny the lovely Indian gloves died on Saturday and Jack was truly sad. They had become great friends. A couple of weeks ago, she gave him a marvelous old print of an albatross saying he would always be reminded of what she had been to him whenever he looked at it.

Last night a group of people met here that are interested in trying to save Midway from being overdeveloped. We talked for hours about whether or not to annex the interchange. We don't particularly want it but are afraid of what could happen out there if we have no control. I'm confused as to what I want. We decided to ask the Mayor to call a special meeting to discuss it.

We received our National Trust Magazine from England today and the front page was a photo of beautiful Petworth Park, which is being "threatened by a dual carriageway". I guess problems are the same all over. We keep hoping that "progress' can become a word which means preserving the charm of a place, rather than pouring concrete over the lovely land.

JUNE 29TH

The Midway Bicentennial is over! And it was a huge success. Ann T and I walked down at nine a.m., and we came home absolutely exhausted at nine tonight. We both had on long, old-fashioned skirts and we loved being part of the act. There was no trouble as John Willie rode around all day on his horse, and we guessed that between four and five thousand people went through during the course of the day.

Thursday night we had Bob and Emily (Biddle), Ben and Ruth, and Alex down and it was very pleasant. The whole thing just might work out.

JULY 1ST

Bob starts in the office today—hope it's going to work.

JULY 4TH

It is the first Fourth of July since we came here in 1959 that none of us are going to the Hicks' pool. Niesje no longer lives out there. Quite a tradition has vanished from our lives. We are going to Pisgah Church for their celebration at six, and it will be lovely, but not the same as Hicks' pool.

Tuesday was our big city council meeting and nothing was decided. We are still up in the air as to what is best for our town.

Last night we went to Ben and Ruth's along with the Biddles and Alex. Everyone got along famously—they are a very compatible group.

JULY 16TH

Early this morning the hospital called Jack saying Miss Amanda Hicks had died. She had a stroke Sunday and her entire left side was paralyzed. She was a great lady.

The first summer that we were here I was lonely and by myself a lot as Jack was gone simply all the time and I was tied down with two small children. Miss Amanda lived in the log cabin behind us and she would sit in the yard with us for hours. She found sitters for me, knit sweaters for Matt (he was soon best friends with her grandson R.W.) and later on she had Matt and R.W. spend the night with her. She would allow the boys to cook, and the next day they would go home with the cookies or Mulligan stew along with the recipe copied carefully in their own handwriting.

All four of our children called her "Granny" and wanted to go to her funeral. They sent her a small basket of yellow roses with a card enclosed that said, "To Granny, with love from Jenny, Matt, Peter and Ann T." She was a very strong lady, but I never felt like she completely got over the death of her son Bob.

JULY 17TH

Ben is down and they are chatting away in the living room trying to plot out the future of the office. It will never cease.

They come up with scheme after scheme to try to improve their schedules, and always end up at square one. The patients are so used to "the Practice" as it has always been and the doctors never have any time to implement their new ideas, so after a few days of doing something new, they fall back into their old routine, every single time.

JULY 24TH

Miss Elizabeth (McCowan) Lehman was in the office yesterday for a regular checkup when Ben found a huge aneurysm in her abdomen. He sent her immediately to Lexington to check with the surgeon, Dick Crutcher.

I had a real scare last night. I was cooking supper late when the back screen door flew open and in charged two teenaged boys, really in a state. I jumped back startled, and they managed to garble out that they had to have Jack instantly—they had seen a man stumble and fall near the office door and they were afraid he might be dead. Jack went running out with them and the man was still there looking like he was in great pain with his face ashen.

They were able to get him into the office where Jack rolled up the man's sleeve in preparation of giving him a shot of Demerol. To Jack's dismay, the arm was marked with the tiny tell-tale scars of a drug user. Jack refused to give him a shot and told him to sit up so they could talk. The man pulled himself together, rolled down his sleeve, his face became a normal color, and he walked out of the office as straight as an arrow. The boys could not believe their eyes. Jack still cannot figure out how he managed the ashen face.

I can remember another drug user who came to the office late one afternoon several years ago. He said he was driving through the countryside and had been stricken with an apparent kidney stone and needed something for pain. He said he was a cousin to the Rockefellers and the girls could call to check out his story if they wanted. They were totally taken in by him until Jack exposed the marks on his arm and told him to get packing. At this time there was a federal narcotics hospital just down the road from us, and the man finally admitted he was on his way to check himself in there and was just trying to have one final fling before going in. He shook Jack's hand and left quietly. On the way out, he admitted that he had no connection with the Rockefellers.

JULY 28TH

We went up to see Miss Elizabeth in St. Joe's. Dick Crutcher operated on her for almost six hours Friday removing the aneurysm and replacing a lot of the occluded synthetic arteries in her legs. Her heart withstood the shock (so far) and she is doing OK. She will be in intensive care for a few days, but Jack can go in to see her.

AUGUST 13TH

Jack pierced Jenny's ears tonight. No comment.

SEPTEMBER 15TH

Jack and I rode over to a house and farm Thursday afternoon that Bob and Emily are thinking about buying. It was exactly twenty miles (or thirty-three minutes) from the office in the opposite direction from the hospital. The present owner had started restoring it, so it has been rewired and replastered. The woodwork is magnificent being paneled and reeded, and the molding is great. The house is "L" shaped and about one hundred and fifty years old. It is a beautiful old place but, in my opinion, it is entirely too far away for him to practice the kind of medicine Jack and Ben do here in Midway.

SEPTEMBER 25TH

Bob Biddle has bid on the farm over in the next county.

SEPTEMBER 30TH

Jack had planned to go to Louisville to medical meetings to get his required hours but two of his OBs went into labor, so he stayed home. Both delivered girls. The big Midway zoning meeting was Thursday night and there was much arguing around. When the dust settled it was agreed that four or five interested citizens will meet and rework the plan by November.

OCTOBER 2ND

Bob got the farm that he had bid on and it is too bad. It will take them entirely out of our community and its affairs.

Alex started back yesterday, and Ben brought the office girls corsages to try to smooth over the fact that they will be doing even more work.

OCTOBER 17TH

Miss Fan Martin died yesterday. Another landmark is gone. She had just turned ninety years old.

OCTOBER 23RD

Jack woke me at six a.m. saying the Clark house in the subdivision that Windy and Jimmy are in the process of building was burning. When I looked out the back window, fire was from one cornice to the other along the top line of the house. Fire fighters were there, but they couldn't get the pressure up for a good stream of water. We threw on jeans and ran up the hill, along with all kinds of other people. Kenney Harper was openly crying, and we all thought it would burn to the ground. Two more fire engines arrived from Versailles, and they were able to get the pressure up. They got the fire out in an hour, but there was extensive damage.

Windy was on the roof while it was burning, and he had a garden hose trying to put out the flames. Jack was a lot more concerned about him than about the house.

NOVEMBER 14TH

When I got up this morning, I put on an old sweatshirt and jeans so I could scrub the kitchen floor. I moved all the furniture out into the dining room and scrubbed on my hands and knees. Just as I finished the door knocker sounded, and I answered it thinking it was a patient. There stood Roberta House from Lehman's shop with a very attractive blonde lady, and Roberta said, "Jonelle, this is the wife of the Governor of Tennessee and she would like to see your lighting fixtures and your kitchen floor. She and her husband are planning to build a house when he gets out of office."

I couldn't believe this had happened when I was so sweaty and dirty, and the house was a total mess. There was nothing to do but laugh and invite her in. She was delightful and most complimentary of the house.

DECEMBER 8TH

Jack ran up to see Miss Elizabeth at St. Joe's in Lexington. She still has about a fifty percent loss of movement in her right side, and he thinks that is pretty long for it to stay if it is going away.

DECEMBER 10TH

Yesterday was Miss Mayme's ninety-eighth birthday, and Jack and I sent her a corsage. Jim was having a dinner for her with all the older folks and we thought she might like to wear flowers.

DECEMBER 15TH

Jack is now jogging three miles every other day, rain or shine. He does it around ten-thirty at night in the new subdivision so no one can see him, and that is seven and one-half boring times over the hill to Windy's lot.

DECEMBER 17TH

A forty-five-year-old patient of Jack's has advanced cancer, so he found out today. She has a sixteen-year-old daughter who is planning to get married in February. Jack had to tell this devastating news to her husband tonight at the hospital, but she was asleep so he will have to tell her and her young daughter tomorrow. This is one of the real heartaches of being a doctor.

Ahead of the Hounds

1975

"Body of Christ. Call the emergency room."

—Father Joe Stephas

JANUARY 8TH

Miss Elizabeth is home and looking better. Jack and I wanted to take her for a short walk today, but she was afraid to try. Her hand is still limp, and I think that is driving her crazy. John Milton wrote that it is not miserable to be blind, it is miserable to be incapable of enduring blindness. I think this concept applies to Miss Elizabeth—she is incapable of enduring that limp hand.

JANUARY 12TH

What a great day! Snow!!! It is almost three inches deep tonight and still coming down. We walked to the Christian Church for a chili supper—the whole family—and it was exhilarating. The snow was beautiful coming down, very fine flakes, and it felt dry and crunchy under our feet.

JANUARY 15TH

After supper we watched TV with the kids until Jack got an emergency call from someone saying that their baby was "acting funny." He went immediately, and the baby was having a bad convulsion. Jack was able to stop it and went with them to the hospital.

JANUARY 22ND

We have just come home from a great dinner party at the Biddles'. Ben, Ruth, Alex and I all drove over in my very compact Comet and it was fun—Jack met us there as he had had a home visit. Ben entertained all the way over telling about some of the unusual house calls in the past. He told about one night years ago when he had to make a home visit on a man who lived on the other side of Frankfort, and he was not sure of the address. He followed the road he thought was right, but he came upon a body of water right in the path of the road, so he turned around and drove back to Frankfort to check at a filling station. They told him that he had been right, and he should go back, drive around the water, and go a few miles on down the road, and he would come to that man's house.

He did as he was told and, sure enough, just on the other side of the water, the road turned into a narrow lane and continued. He came to a closed gate. He got out of the car, opened the gate, got back in the car, drove through, got out of the car and closed the gate, got back in and drove on.

On down the lane a little way, he came to another closed gate, and he repeated the procedure. He found two more closed gates, which he opened and closed until he was blue in the face, but by now he was determined that he would find that house or die in the attempt, so he pressed on.

At the end of the lane there stood a small house with a porch light on. He got out of the car and reached into the back seat to get his medical bag and it was not there. He had left it at the office. With heroic patience, he got back in the car and returned to the office for his bag, going through all those gates and all those openings and closing and came back once again.

Years later, he said, when he wasn't so young and foolish, a similar incident occurred, and he went in the house the first time he arrived and bluffed his way through. He took the man's pulse, listened to his chest and his back with his ear placed flat on that patient's body and asked his wife if he could borrow a spoon in order to check the throat.

Ben is most delightful when he is telling stories. He got that trait from his Daddy.

JANUARY 24TH

We built a fire in the den fireplace and Jack and I sat in front of it and talked until midnight. We hadn't talked like that in a very long time. Overdue.

FEBRUARY 8TH

Monsignor Hillenmeyer died yesterday—he was ninety-seven, and his old body just gave out. He has said the Masses at Taylor Manor for the past several years as he has been living there. He genuflected at every appropriate time and was always clear as a bell. We have been going to Mass there on Christmas mornings at six and the children have always loved Monsignor Hillenmeyer, considering him to be our own Father Christmas.

Last year as we were going home, Jenny was thinking about the fact that he was so old and she said, "Gee, I'll miss him when he's gone."

Matt, wide-eyed and indignant asked, "What do you mean Jenny? Where is he going?"

APRIL 11TH

A lady patient of Jack's cut her hand off with a butcher knife because she thought she heard the Lord tell her to do it. Jack said it was absolutely ghastly. The hand was there on the kitchen table when he went in, and he had to pick it up and put it in a pan of iced salt water and send it to the hospital in hopes that the surgeons could reattach it to her wrist. He couldn't get to sleep tonight as he couldn't get her off his mind.

APRIL 22ND

Jack told me last night that Alex has applied for a job with HEW in Washington, D.C. Really hate to see him leave the county but Jack said he was excited about the prospect of the job.

A mildly retarded man called on the phone nine times after midnight last night worried about his mother. Finally, at four a.m. Jack called for the ambulance to take her to the hospital. Can't imagine who will take care of her son while she is gone. He called back at six a.m. to tell us that he was going to trade in his car for an organ with a drum attached to the side. He is a very sweet and gentle man, and we worry that he will get hurt living alone.

APRIL 24TH

Jack invited his Sunday School class of twelve teenagers over for a cookout and asked Alex's class from the Presbyterian

Church to join them. We called Tom Jones (from Versailles) and a friend to come and play their guitars for entertainment. I did not know most of the children that came but I thought I would not be too involved since Jack and Alex had promised to be here all evening. I should have known better.

At six-fifteen it was pouring rain and eighteen teenagers arrived. Jack moved the grill inside the garage and put on the first round of hamburgers before he had to leave to deliver a baby. Alex drove up as Jack was backing out the driveway and cut the brownies for me before leaving to make home visits. I was left with the boys and girls who did not know me at all, and did not know each other very well, and the rain was coming down even harder. I put Jenny in charge of the grill and told the two guitarists to hit it. It was a long evening.

MAY 16TH

We were taking Jenny and Matt to see the play "Godspell" at the dinner theatre tonight because they both had earned such good grades. But Jack called at five-fifteen saying that he had an OB in and we would have to go without him. The three of us were crushed but the play was so wonderful that it almost compensated for our disappointment.

MAY 20TH

An old Frankenstein movie was on TV tonight and Jack wanted to watch it with the children. It reminded me of the summer we moved to Midway and there was a movie house in Versailles called "The Bard". One rainy Sunday afternoon, "The Bride of Frankenstein" was showing and Jack had talked me into getting a sitter and going with him to see it as he has a real weakness for those old things. We went in with the hordes of kids and the few parents who had been pressed into coming by their children.

The movie had barely started when the screen went dark, the house lights went up, and the manager walked briskly to the center of the stage, "Dr. Fisher!" he shouted dramatically. "Dr. Fisher! You have an emergency at the hospital, and you are to go there immediately!" He put his hands above his eyes to shield them from the lights and kept looking for Jack until he saw us sitting there mortified. We were caught and new enough to the community to be embarrassed to be seen, without children, at a Frankenstein movie. As we stumbled out red-faced, the lights went off and we could hear the soundtrack come on again.

MAY 23RD

There was a violent storm tonight, but Jack and I went to Levas' for dinner anyway. We got in a big argument over the stupid boat while we were there and it spoiled our evening out. While I was in Berea today with Peter's class on a field trip. Jack went to Shelbyville to see about his boat and he brought the thing back home with him along with the motor, which was in a hundred pieces. Last spring the motor was acting up, so on "Eddie's" recommendation we took it to a man in Shelbyville who had said the motor would be in "new condition" for two hundred and fifty dollars and ready for the water before summer was over. As it is, he kept the boat for twelve months, charged Jack five hundred dollars, and sent the motor back in pieces—not worth a Continental. Now we have paid five hundred dollars, our motor is worthless, we have missed two seasons in the water, and Jack thinks he is a great guy. We had a huge row, and I am not sure who won.

MAY 27TH

Peter, Ann T and I left home at the crack of dawn pulling that dumb boat with us to see what our options were. We sat cooling our heels one and a half hours waiting for Eddie, our boat man in Frankfort. As many times as I have been in this marina, I have never heard his last name. Finally, he sauntered in—said he would put the motor back together again, if it ran, fine. If it didn't, we were out of luck. But either way he would not charge us anything. He must have seen how desperate I was, or he felt horribly guilty for recommending that Shelbyville man to us.

It has been heart breaking to watch Jack getting discouraged with his boat—then frustrated—then depressed. When he was unloading the junk from it this morning in the drizzling rain, I felt unbearably sorry for him. He loves the river and the old boat, and he spends so very little money on himself. So on the spur of the moment, I asked Eddie how much a fifty horsepower motor would cost new and if he would give us a good trade. Turns out he would. But it will still be a hefty sum. I felt like I had to check it out with Jack. When I asked him at lunch, he looked just like a kid—I loved it—and it was worth any financial sacrifice.

MAY 29TH

Bruce Davis, our good friend, called to see if he and his wife (Patsy) might come down awhile after supper last night. They arrived around eight-thirty, and we had a wonderful time just chatting until around midnight. Then Bruce remarked casually "Doctor-Friend, I think I might have had a heart attack on Monday." It was said nonchalantly but we could tell he was concerned. He had been throwing bales of hay when his arms and chest started hurting and he rested. The hurting did not go away so he went home. That night he finally went to sleep on his stomach on a huge pillow and when he woke up at three-thirty a.m. the hurting had stopped. He mowed grass on Tuesday and felt OK. Jack said he should come to the office the next day to have an EKG, but he sort of scoffed it off. For some unknown reason, I insisted that we go to the office right then and there at midnight so Jack could do it then.

When Jack did the EKG it was totally haywire. He called a friend in Midway, Russ McAllister, who is a heart specialist, for a verification of the reading because it looked so bad. Both Jack and Russ agreed that Bruce had had a major coronary and should be hospitalized immediately.

Jack and I followed Bruce and Pat to the hospital where they hooked him to a monitor and watched him very closely. Because of being so emotionally involved with a good friend, Jack was afraid he might have neglected to do something, so he called Alex (it was now three-thirty a.m.) to check what he had done, and Alex assured him that he had done everything right.

We were home by three-forty-five but I still could not go to sleep. You just do not think about things like this happening to people you know and love. Bruce is such a gentle, kind, generous human being—my best friend—for ten years. He is only forty-seven years old.

This evening Patsy called to say that Bruce had had a pretty good day and was terribly proud that he had not smoked a cigarette all day. Jack's having to deal with telling Bruce last night reminded me of the time when he had to tell Bob Hicks about the malignant spot on his lung. It is just bone-deep bad. Being a "Doctor-Friend" isn't much fun—it can break your heart.

MAY 31ST

Peter and Ann T are playing "Club" with Leighton and Chris (Riddle Brothers) two kids on the block, and they are out in the new tent. Peter just came in to ask if we had a fan that could run on batteries—he was as hot as fire with sweat running down his neck.

JUNE 12TH

Last Sunday when it came time to take Communion, I was standing just in front of Jack. Joe Stephas, the priest, said to me, "Body of Christ." Whereupon I responded "Amen" and took the Host.

As I was crossing myself, I heard Father Joe's voice repeat to Jack, "Body of Christ." Then, in the exact same low tone he added, "Call the emergency room." I felt like I had witnessed a James Bond drop as I watched Jack head for the back door instead of our pew.

When Jack told Ben about this incident, Ben said a couple of weeks ago during the sermon at the Christian Church, the back door flew open and a man came in waving his arms, wide-eyed, and calling loudly for Doctor Roach. Ben jumped up and ran out expecting to find a person in really dire straights only to find out that the man's wife had something in her eye. He was almost embarrassed to go back in church. I guess the patients feel like church is the one place where they have the doctor treed.

JULY 20TH

We were getting dressed for the Benjamin's lovely horse sales party when Jack got a distress call from the Lehmans.

Miss Elizabeth was vomiting and spitting up blood, so Jack took off. He rode to St. Joe's in the ambulance with her because he really doubted she'd make it. They got there OK and she was stabilized when he left. We were forty-five minutes late to the party and no one seemed to notice.

JULY 25TH

Last night I asked Matt to take out the garbage and he answered, "Sure, Mom."

Half an hour later, the garbage was still sitting there, and I blew my stack. I very seldom ask the children to do much around the house and I expect them to comply immediately when I do. So I lambasted Matt with a tirade all while he was tying up the bag and as he drug it out of the kitchen. Jack (who had been sitting at the table the entire time) grinned at me and said, "Well, Jo, you have said it all. You left yourself nothing to say should he ever come home high on marijuana." I had to admit that he was right.

JULY 27TH

Miss Elizabeth died around eight this morning and I am truly sad. It was she, more than anyone, who taught me what is interesting about antiques and who helped us with this house. She was exactly what she was—and regardless of the consequences, she was not about to change. I like that. I feel like a legend is gone.

AUGUST 14TH

Jack and I went to the beautiful Kentucky River at eleven-thirty and had a lovely day alone. Came home at four.

AUGUST 16TH

Ironed all day getting Jenny ready to go to college. Came to her old blue denim skirt that she has been wearing all summer, and I started crying. It is the first break up of our family circle and it is hard to face up to. She is such a part of our lives that it will be difficult for all of us to be the same when she is gone. I hope she knows how very much we care for her—surely she does.

AUGUST 20TH

The hospital is having a hard time. Last night the Board decided to fire the administrator (who had been there for nine years), and their head nurse. Hope they don't let the doctors go.

AUGUST 30TH

Ben called Jack at eight-o-clock this morning to tell him that Mr. Tom had died at Taylor Manor. I had forgotten how much I loved him. The body and the service will be at Ben's house at the farm, the burial will be in Lexington Cemetery. He was so wonderful to me when I needed it so many years ago. He used to come and visit once or twice a week, telling tales of old Midway and entertaining the children. He had a couple of strokes about five years ago and has been living at Taylor Manor ever since. A very wealthy man, who never seemed to lose the common touch. I loved him.

LABOR DAY, SEPTEMBER 1ST

We buried Mr. Tom today and I positively wept. Bill McDonald, the Christian church minister, gave the eulogy and it was very moving. He said Mr. Tom had been so many things to so many people and he had touched so many of us with his life. It was true for me—I simply adored him. The pall bearers were his grandsons and two men who had worked for him for years. Jack was an honorary pall bearer along with about a dozen more. We went to the burial in Lexington and that was the only thing I would have changed. If ever a human belonged in Midway, it was Mr. Tom.

SEPTEMBER 4TH

Ruth called to say that Mr. Owen Rouse died last night, also in Taylor Manor. He was Mr. Tom's best buddy and the two of them used to take Jack and me to the races frequently. We went with them even to Cincinnati and Louisville the year "Red Jonelle" ran. Really sad that they would be buried in the same month.

SEPTEMBER 16TH

We are having dinner tonight to meet the two new surgeons that the hospital has recruited. Bob, Emily, and Alex are coming also.

OCTOBER 7TH

Alex says the Health Board met with the Zoning Board and they decided that a house in the country needs only two and a half acres to install a septic tank. Wish it were more like it used to be.

OCTOBER 17TH

Wednesday night Jack and I went to show our slides of our trip out west to Mrs. Margaret Foster and Miss Helen

McKinley who are two of his elderly patients. They were all dressed up in silk dresses and even had on lipstick. They thoroughly enjoyed the slides, then Jack worked on Mrs. Margaret's leg while Miss Helen took me on a tour of her part of the house. That place is enormous. I loved the upstairs porch—it was raining and just delightful.

Friday, we went to the Woman's Club Spaghetti Supper, and it was delicious. We sat with Ben, and he said his son Tommy may be moving into Mr. Tom's old house. It looks like it needs a lot of work. Ben and the farmhands had cleaned the yard all day.

OCTOBER 23RD

Jim and Port Rouse gave us a Cherokee Princess white dogwood tree to celebrate the birth of their son, Jonathan. Jack delivered him and they are very proud. Jim even came with his shovel and planted it for us.

OCTOBER 28TH

Got the kids off this morning and then Jack and I went to get the boat out of the river for the winter. It was a mess at the dock as the water was high and debris was floating all around. Jack got trapped in the boat behind a dock but was finally able to push his way through and arrived in Frankfort forty-five minutes late. We left the boat with Eddie for its winterizing. Wonder how much that will set us back.

NOVEMBER 15TH

Alex told Jack today that he is leaving the practice as of January first because it is driving him crazy. He said that obviously he is not cut out for general practice and right now he is having doubts that he is meant for medicine at all. Jack and I are devoted to Alex and want his happiness above all else. We simply can't imagine the office without him now as he brought a wonderful sense of humor to the whole thing. We will miss him.

NOVEMBER 22ND

One of Jack's old lady patients has started calling several times during the night—every night—and it is driving me up the wall. Last night she called three times after midnight because she couldn't sleep. She lives by herself, and I guess gets scared and wants the security of knowing she can get Jack anytime she needs him. Anyway, on the third time I came to the couch in the den so I wouldn't bother Jack with my tossing and turning. I was also planning on grabbing the phone whenever she called again.

NOVEMBER 28TH

Wednesday noon we went to the Midway Christian Church for the Thanksgiving Market Luncheon. Always the same, oyster stew, chicken salad, and pie. Always delicious. I sat with the office staff and enjoyed. Thought all day about Mr. Tom as I used to sit with him every year.

DECEMBER 18TH

When we had the office staff down for a chili lunch last week, we got to teasing Ben about the house call he made on the horse farm lady where he ate supper at home and then had to eat the supper she fed him not thirty minutes later. He said the worst thing about it was that the very next time he made a home visit on her he wanted to draw blood to run tests. He meticulously cleaned off her middle finger and then pricked her ring finger by mistake. He was embarrassed when she asked why he did that.

DECEMBER 24TH

Sunday we had a party for Jack's older patients who have been so wonderful to us all these years. Twenty-eight people came and our children behaved beautifully for once. Jenny and one of her friends poured the punch and the eggnog for us. Ann T was dressed in a long skirt to greet the guests at the door. Matt and Peter had on ties, and they took people's coats and brought them back as they were needed. Everything ran smoothly and I believe the guests enjoyed seeing the house all decorated and being with children at Christmastime.

Ahead of the Hounds

1976

"I'm not coming Ella!"

—Jack

JANUARY 1ST

We went to two small parties last night but were home by twelve to sip a taste of champagne with Jenny and Matt. We watched TV with them until one a.m. This morning a man knocked at the door loudly three separate times before seven wanting Jack, so everybody in the house was up by seven-thirty and we were in time for early Mass.

JANUARY 5TH

On Friday around three-thirty in the afternoon, our old friend OB Wilder had a terrible time—turning blue and in great pain. Jack left the office to ride in the ambulance with him to St. Joe's in Lexington because he was not sure he was going to make it. He has now rallied, and the crisis seems to be over.

JANUARY 10TH

Jack took Peter and Ann T ice skating, and they loved being with their Dad doing anything. The ponds hadn't been frozen over hard for so long that it made it a special occasion. I walked up to the grocery to buy hot dogs and marshmallows which we roasted over the den fire for supper when the skaters came in. Ann T and Peter couldn't believe we were cooking in the den.

JANUARY 15TH

We visited OB Wilder today—he is home from the hospital but can't go walking for five weeks. He is accustomed to walking at least two hours every day all over town, telling everyone "the news". This inactivity will drive him crazy.

Jack started to jog at ten tonight, ran four miles, took a sauna and bath, and was ready to go to sleep. He is getting into better and better shape while I deteriorate before my very eyes.

JANUARY 18TH

Matt false started twice in a swimming meet at Ashland, Kentucky last night and received his first disqualification ever. He was devastated until Jack told him that he was the only kid there who was faster than the gun. He finally managed a grin on that one.

Parents at these meets are not to be believed. One man yelled loudly at this little girl, "Come on Helen! Win the damned thing!" Another man ran up and down the side of the pool during a nine-ten year old boys' competition, screaming, "Kick, Preston! Kick, kick, kick Preston!" Preston finally stood stock still on the bottom of the pool, with his crew cut positively bristling, and hollered back, "I AM kicking!!!" Then he put his head back down and finished the race—dead last.

JANUARY 23RD

We went to Jim Cogar's for supper and two or three inches of snow were on the ground. We went for a walk around the fields and gloried in the sunset over the snow. After dinner we read a diary that had belonged to his Aunt Edna—it was written in 1894. They lived in town and the girls would walk down the streets several times a day, sleep all afternoon and be ready to go again at night. Her sister, Miss Mayme, was eighteen and constantly referred to as "Dear Mayme."

FEBRUARY 5TH

On Tuesday at six o-clock, Jack was stuck at the hospital, so I drove Ann Lewis and Ruth to the office party at the dinner theatre. "Godspell" was still showing. Jack's patient has flu pneumonia and they are all afraid she will die. Because of this there was little jocularity at our table. Jack kept running in and out all evening and was on the phone half the time. The show was excellent once again, but it didn't seem important to us.

FEBRUARY 13TH

Jack's patient died this morning of viral pneumonia and her husband asked Jack to please tell the children, aged eleven, eight and fourteen. The mom had been thirty-five years old. So much for Friday the thirteenth.

FEBRUARY 16TH

Went to bed with a cough at ten and coughed until Jack came in at eleven-forty-five from delivering a baby. I came down to the kitchen and drank a special concoction of lemon juice, bourbon and honey and went right to sleep. I should patent that recipe. Ella Wright woke us both up at six-o'clock and we considered ourselves lucky that it wasn't five.

FEBRUARY 18TH

Jack had to go on a home visit last night to see Margaret Foster. After he had taken care of her leg, she told him that she had been planning on going on a Caribbean cruise along with a companion, and now that she didn't feel up to it, she wanted us to go in their places. She had written a check for him, and he was genuinely touched by her generosity. To his credit, he refused to even look at the check much less accept it. She is a great lady.

MARCH 24TH

Bruce Davis came by while I was reading "King Lear" in the yard. He is down to four cigarettes a day and is miserable. I love to talk to him about books—he is probably the most intelligent person I have ever known.

APRIL 3RD

Yesterday Ella Wright called for Jack at ten after four and woke us up. This was the fifth day that she had done this. I couldn't go back to sleep, so I came down to the den and read "King Lear" until it was time to fix breakfast. Jack and Ben can both go back to sleep instantly no matter how many times they are called. Ben tells of the time when he went to bed exhausted at midnight, only to be awakened at three a.m. by a lady wanting a home visit. He told her that he would be right there—then he promptly fell back asleep with the phone cradled against his ear. The lady survived albeit pretty angry when he just didn't show up and his phone line remained busy so she couldn't call again to get him. The ability to fall right back to sleep after being awakened is a gift from God, and luckily, they are both endowed with it.

APRIL 8TH

Jack was on call again, went to the hospital to deliver a baby and came home at three a.m. Ella Wright called at five for a home visit and Jack shouted in the phone "I'm not coming Ella!" and went back to sleep. Maybe there is hope for him yet. (Way in the back of my mind is a nagging little voice that says one of these mornings, Ella's complaint will be real, and no one will hurry to her side because she has hollered "wolf" too often.)

Jack had to leave anyway at six o-clock to see a possible heart attack. Quite a night.

MIDNIGHT, APRIL 15TH

Billy Moore just called a minute ago for Jack to see his wife Joyce, as they thought their son Charlie had just been killed in a car accident. I am utterly heartsick.

Jenny started in the first grade with Charlie, and they stayed together in the same class throughout high school. His mom and dad are great people in our church. What a tragedy. I think I'll read until Jack comes home, as he is bound to want to talk.

APRIL 16TH

When Jack got to the Moore's last night, no one was sure it had been Charlie in the accident. Two boys in a pick-up truck were passing two other boys and their dates on US 33. The driver lost control of the truck and it smashed into a tree on a curve. This boy was pulled from the vehicle, then it caught fire, exploded, and the passenger was burned beyond recognition. While Jack was there trying to calm an almost hysterical mother, one of the other boys arrived and told the Moore's that yes, it had been Charlie. It is a nightmare.

APRIL 17TH

Jack took our family to Frankfort to McDonalds for supper, then he and I went to the funeral home for Charlie Moore. It was unbearably sad. We talked to Joyce and Billy, and she cried when remembering Charlie and Jenny's days at St. Leo's Elementary School. Joyce said she could cope with his death if she just knew the reason it had to happen. She and Billy both have a tremendous faith in God, and that is bound to carry them through the next few weeks. They had put his big high school graduation picture beside a closed casket. Charlie was enormously popular in school and all sorts of young people were there. It was a very emotional time.

APRIL 30TH

The huge test Jack must take in October to renew his qualification in the family practice field is going to be held in Denver, San Francisco, New York or New Orleans. The cost is one hundred and fifty dollars not counting the trip. He had to mail the check back immediately so we could get our choice of New Orleans.

JUNE 12TH

Yesterday, the Midway Bank was robbed of eight thousand, five hundred dollars in broad daylight by two bandits! They phoned the jeans factory with a hoax bomb threat, and when the police raced down there, the masked robbers slipped into the bank and demanded the cash. They made a complete getaway.

JUNE 22ND

Around six p.m. yesterday, Jack had to make a home visit on Margaret Foster. She called for me to come along and we would celebrate Jack's birthday. After Jack checked her leg, we went back to the dining room along with Miss Foster and Miss Helen McKinlay. Miss Helen lit five candles that were in the center of the table, which were in the middle of an arrangement of daisies. Jack poured the sherry, and we had olives, nuts, crackers and Liederkranz cheese. Their gift to him was a delicious chocolate pie—his favorite. They were all dressed up in their silk dresses. We ate on bicentennial plates, and everything matched. It was very touching that they had gone to so much trouble for him. Miss Margaret admitted that she was forty-four when Jack was born—that makes her eighty-eight now, and Miss Helen is eighty-four. They are two very special people.

This morning we were up early. Jack got a call at six from an OB who was in labor, and at six-fifteen, a man called with a possible coronary—at six-thirty, Jack ran by the office to pick up the man's chart, only to find that the office had been broken into and ransacked by someone looking for drugs we suppose. What a way to start a day.

JUNE 26TH

We gave a dinner party for Ben and Ruth's son, Jimmy, who is getting married next month. It had to be the worst party we have ever given, and probably the worst that we have ever been to. No reflection on the guests—just nothing clicked, and the food was not good. We had planned an hour for cocktails, but no one was drinking—not even juice or ginger ale—and somehow conversations were slow. I ran into the kitchen to hurry up the food and the rice ended up overcooked while the chicken did not get done. We gave toasts for the young couple and Jack accidentally knocked over his glass of red wine and it went all over the bride's father who is a county elected official and teetotaler. When Coemma loaded the dishwasher after dinner, water started spewing out beneath the sink like the Niagara Falls. The whole pipe had burst, and Jenny, Matt, Coemma, Tommy Roach (who had wandered out to the kitchen) and I mopped up with big swim towels for half an hour. It was not a night to brag about.

When I told Jim Cogar about it later, he said it reminded him of a party he had given in Williamsburg, which for some reason just "didn't go." He had gone tearing out to the kitchen to tell his cook, Robina, to hurry things up and she had made the poignant remark, "What's the matter out there tonight, Mr. Cogar? You are asking all the questions and giving all the answers." Exactly. I could not have possibly described my evening any better.

JUNE 28TH

Jack left to go to the hospital tonight right after we saw the night-blooming primroses at Margaret Ware's. They are fascinating. Around sundown they literally burst into brilliant yellow blooms—like a time exposure camera shot, and they stay until sunrise at which time they wilt. The children loved them and would race from one to another as they popped into bloom.

JULY 1ST

Jack's day off and he cleaned on his boat until three, then we headed with it to the Kentucky River. After backing the trailer beautifully down the ramp and dislodging the boat into the water, we found that the motor would not turn over. We then tried six times to load the thing back on the trailer and it kept slipping off the traces. Finally, by both of us tugging and pushing with all our might, it slipped into place. We took it to "Eddie's" and dumped it.

Peter, Ann T and Jack made vanilla ice cream tonight, and it was worth all the trouble they went to trying to make it freeze.

JULY 23RD

The motor is fixed so we took Peter and Ann T to the river. It was searing hot so we were home by four.

Day before yesterday Jack came in very tense and weary, as he had had another horrible day at the office. He had delivered a baby who was six weeks early and was not breathing right. There was not a respirator to be had in Lexington, so he had to send the baby down to Louisville. An old patient that Jack particularly loved had died. Our neighbor has a "stone" that they can't dislodge by the "below" method and they have to do the "above" surgery, and Jack had trouble trying to set this up. Some days it gets to him more than others.

AUGUST 25TH

Matt and I drove Jenny down to Bowling Green to Western Kentucky University and I hated to leave her because she was going just to please her daddy and me. She had declared that she didn't want to go on to school but to get a job instead. Jack and I had encouraged her to go at least one more year and she reluctantly agreed to try Western. When it became time to take her, Jack had an OB in so I drafted Matt to come along in his place. We moved her into the dorm, and it was time for us to go home. When she turned to wave good-bye, she was sobbing and I asked through my own tears, "Matt, what in the world are we going to do?"

"Gun it, Mom! It is the only way," he replied. I gunned it.

SEPTEMBER 8TH

Bruce Davis came down on Tuesday night admitting to Jack that he drinks too often and asking for help. I have been in a state of depression ever since as he is the best friend I ever had, and I don't know how to help him.

SEPTEMBER 10TH

Things have been grim for the Davis family, but so far so good. Bruce is trying to kick the habit on his own and has had all the shakes and other problems plus, I'm sure the relentless desire for another drink. Do hope and pray he makes it. We went by there Wednesday night, and he looked like the 'wrath of God'. Jack has been stopping by every morning and every evening and things seem as good as could be expected.

SEPTEMBER 16TH

The City Council voted Monday night to annex property along US 421 but not to include a nearby portion of the interstate.

OCTOBER 14TH

Bad news. Bob Biddle told Jack he is looking elsewhere for a place to practice. That he does not want to spend the rest of his life like this. It is partly that farm and partly Emily wanting him home more and partly resentment that he has no time to call his own, even on weekends when he is not on call. I feel sorry for Bob, but desperately sorry for Jack and Ben, as the practice is too big to be handled without Bob. Jack is delivering a baby tonight and I am trying to stay awake until he comes in.

OCTOBER 24TH

OB Wilder came in for a few minutes and a cup of coffee. We discussed politics and books, both of which I stand in awe of his knowledge.

Jack was upset Friday night because the parents of a fourteen-year-old girl had stopped him in the hospital saying that the child had been with an undesirable boy all afternoon and they wanted Jack to find out if she had "had relations."

Jack talked to the girl, and she admitted that she had, but that she was pregnant by another boy at school. The parents are beside themselves. Jack told them to all go home for the weekend and talk until they had settled some big issues, if he could help them on Monday, for them to call. They were Dr. Reed's patients and I know Jack hopes they'll get back to him on Monday.

OCTOBER 25TH

Emily Biddle delivered a baby boy this morning—on Peter's twelfth birthday! Peter had a great day. The presents he received were: two car models to add to his collection, a bike, and a Deluxe Mastermind game. Not bad for a twelve-year-old.

NOVEMBER 8TH

Ben approached Jack with a new idea. He said the office had been asked to set up a training unit for the residents of family practice at the University. The first-year four would come, the second year, eight: then there would be twelve from then on, Jack, Ben and Bob would be paid a goodly sum per year to teach these residents in addition to their regular practice income. The residents would all live in Midway, take all night and weekend calls and the University would expand the office and buy all new equipment that was needed. Bob was enthusiastic, Jack was appalled.

This would change the heart and soul of his practice and he loves it as it is. He doesn't want to give up his home visits ever. All he wants to do is see his old patients one at a time, birth their babies, and cure their ills. But how can he ask the other two to pass up the gravy, particularly when he knows Bob is unhappy with things the way they are?

He has decided, as of today, to tell them that he cannot go along, but for them to go full speed ahead without him. That he will try to share the office space practicing as he always has. If it doesn't work out, he will leave the building and just practice here in Midway. We are holding our breaths for the outcome.

NOVEMBER 14TH

Jack is more and more depressed about the office. Bob has said he won't teach the residents if Jack won't go along, and he doesn't understand why Jack doesn't want to do it. Jack looks terrible. It is his first confrontation with Ben since they started working together.

We took OB Wilder to see "The Taming of the Shrew" at the Opera House in Lexington tonight and went to his house afterwards for a nightcap. Jack discussed the office problem with him, and OB was extremely sympathetic. He said he thought Jack should make a break—he should not give up the basic character of his practice for any reason in the world. It is scary and sad to think about. Home by twelve-thirty.

Had supper with Alex this Friday and saw Dustin Hoffman in "The Marathon Man" with him. Alex came in here later and we talked until one a.m. He is going to the Frontier Nursing Hospital in Eastern Ky for six months and he seems happy about it.

NOVEMBER 25TH

The University unit that Ben wanted so much in Midway has by-passed us and has chosen to go to a neighboring county. I do hope Ben is not too disappointed.

CHRISTMAS EVE

The best present of all arrived—Tom Bombadil—a Golden Retriever puppy. I have never seen the kids so happy. He is adorable.

We had our third annual party for our older Midway friends yesterday. It was by far the best—I guess it gets easier the more often you do it. We had wassail (poured by Jenny), eggnog (poured by one of Jenny's friends whose grandmother was one of the guests), seventy-two country ham biscuits, sixty turkey salad sandwiches, cookies from St. Leo's church, cheese straws that Jean Rouse had made for us, candy and a fruit cake from patients, and salted pecans from Margaret Foster and Helen McKinlay. Counting our family, there were thirty-nine of us here, and all the guests were over seventy-years-old. It is our favorite Christmas party.

Bruce Davis has stayed off the bottle, but he is smoking again. Bad for his heart but I guess good for his soul. He can't lick all his problems at once I suppose.

DECEMBER 26TH

Jack came in at three a.m. last night after delivering a girl who was just seven months pregnant, fifteen-years-old, and totally hysterical. She had a three-pound, eleven-ounce baby that seems to be OK.

1977

"This girl has just had a baby in bed,
and I need the doctor."

—Frantic Father

JANUARY 11TH

Our outdoor thermometer registered minus eight degrees this morning and I had to walk to the grocery by the post office because the roads were as slick as glass. Four inches of snow fell Friday, with a winter storm watch out on Saturday and nine more inches of snow fell Sunday. The kids are home from school, tired already of their Christmas games and books. Jack had to go to the Hospital to deliver a baby in the middle of the night—he said he had to creep over the slick roads—and two more pregnant patients called thinking they were in labor, panicked because of the bad roads. He was able to calm them both down on the phone and didn't hear from them again during the night.

JANUARY 26TH

The children are still out of school because of the weather, it will be six weeks on Friday, and they are beside themselves with boredom. We have taken to watch the bird feeder by the hour, and they are elated when a new type appears. Their bright spot of their day yesterday was the Purple Finches, a new variety for Peter and Ann T.

JANUARY 27TH

It is cold and cloudy, snowing in Louisville, and a cold front moving in for tomorrow. I heard today that the Ohio and Kentucky Rivers are frozen over in spots—first time in thirty years. Elderly people have been calling just to have Jack reassure them that he will be nearby and will get out to them if they need him. There is a real feeling of "hunkering down" in the community now and it is not all bad.

JANUARY 28TH

The temperature is six degrees, and it is three o-clock in the afternoon. It is due to drop between minus five and minus ten tonight. The Midway-Versailles Road is closed out at Smiser West's farm with great drifts and several vehicles are stranded out there including one snow plough. If Jack has to go to the hospital tonight, he will have to use the Interstate to Frankfort and then double back.

FEBRUARY 1ST

Twenty-seven degrees today! And it feels like spring. We heard on the radio that Woodford County Schools are called off through Friday because of gas shortage. That will make it seven weeks without school if you count Christmas vacation and provided they do start on Monday. The children have gotten used to their holiday and have started to do schoolwork here and to read a lot. They have been reasonably good, considering.

The gas shortage is real. When we finally went to the mall in Lexington yesterday just for an outing, there was no heat turned on in there at all. They were hoping that the heat from the lights and the people would suffice, and it didn't feel as cold as you might think.

MARCH 4TH

Yesterday, we went to the Frontier Nursing Hospital to visit Alex. He went there on a six-month stint because they desperately needed a doctor, and he was not tied up at the moment, and it was an ancestor of his who had founded the hospital in the first place.

We arrived at noon and had lunch with Alex in the hospital cafeteria—a good pizza. Then we walked outside and met Marcie, a nurse at the hospital and a friend to Alex. She was in charge of a district outside the town, and each nurse with this responsibility is given a jeep to drive to make house visits.

We decided to go on a couple of calls with her and the roads were not to be believed. They were badly paved for about five miles out with huge potholes in them. At the five mile point they became dirt with gravel spots for about one hundred yards, then came water, ruts, and mud for about five more miles. We went into the four-wheel drive about halfway up the mountain side. The ravine was enormous on my side of the road, and I was holding on for dear life as we slid all the way up.

The house we visited first was standing in a yard of mud with chickens all over the place. There were a husband and a wife there—he was seventy-one, blinded by a coal mining accident with a slight case of black lung disease. He had worked the mines for forty years and his hands were blackened by the grit. He said he loved working in the mines and that he had been a man who loaded the coal—that it was the men who drilled that got the black lung so bad.

Cora was seventy-three and complained of "smothering," and that her feet and legs "burned like fire." She and her husband were cousins and had lived in this valley all their lives and had eleven children. The oldest and second to the youngest had died. Once a few years back, five of them had moved to Dayton to work in the factories and had persuaded their parents to come and live with them. They had stayed about five weeks but were homesick for the hills and had returned, leaving the children there.

They had a son who coughed all the time and they thought he had TB. The husband said, "I'm afraid he'll just hump up (die) and it'll look bad on us. We're tryin' to get him to the doctor."

She said, "I'll be better when I can get outside and sweat. Get some of this laziness out of me."

In their house was a potbellied stove, a couch, an overstuffed chair, a bench and two hard chairs. There were pictures everywhere of grandchildren and of Jesus. There was the largest TV that I had ever seen, which I guessed to be a gift from the Dayton group.

They begged us to come back when we were ready to leave and I was truly drawn by their sincerity and warmth. She followed us out of the porch to wave us goodbye, and, as we were getting into the Jeep, she brought out a big black pipe and proceeded to light it. June tenth will be their fiftieth wedding anniversary.

Marci turned the jeep around on a slippery incline that made her sit about two feet higher than I. It never occurred to me but what we would turn over. I did not think we would be hurt because we had a heavy rollbar, and we were practically sitting still but I kept thinking how muddy we would be. However, she made the turn safely and we started back along the Lower Trace.

On the way back we stopped where we had to walk up an enormously steep hill to get to the house. A big pile of coal was at the foot of the hill right beside the road, where Pa had to walk down—seventy-one years old also—and carry up a bucket full whenever it was needed. He has arthritis in his left leg and high blood pressure. He was worried and nervous because one of his sons was in an intensive care unit in Louisville as a result of a car wreck. The other son was in Alex's care at the hospital because of a coal mining accident when he was twenty-three and his leg had become infected and gradually, Pa said, it was "eaten away."

We went in a room at Pa's for Marci to check him. The nurses check the patients here in their homes, and, if they think a doctor is needed, the patient is brought into the hospital. The doctors do not make home visits except in extreme cases. These people all recognized Alex, and were surprised and pleased that he was in their homes.

The room where Pa was lying in bed was spotlessly clean, with two double beds, a stove, three chairs, and another vast array of pictures. These people seem to have a good sense of humor and I guess an inborn sense of gritty intelligence. I liked them on the spot and felt privileged to have been in their homes.

We had supper with Alex at the big old house that had been built in 1925, as two big log cabins with a closed-in dog trot that joined them together. Some others of the staff joined us, and we had a marvelous meal that was set on the huge wooden table, and we passed the food around. We had meatloaf, baked potatoes, squash casserole, green beans, tossed salad and coconut pie. Altogether a delicious feast. They passed great pitchers of milk or water around for us to drink.

It was one of my all-time favorite days and we loved being with Alex. We were home by one in the morning.

MARCH 15TH

Jack told me that they found a spot on OB's lung the size of a fifty-cent piece that did not show up on the 1975 x-ray. OB is in abject despair. His heart specialist is ill, can't see him until Friday when he will have to decide whether or not to operate because OB's heart is so bad. We are holding our breaths until the verdict is in.

The heart specialist says there is no way that OB is to be operated on. Now what?

MARCH 31ST

Went with Jack to Ben and Ruth's for dinner with the entire office staff. They now have six incredible girls on their staff, and we really do enjoy their husbands as well at these outings. Thirteen people were there. We walked back to the barn to see Cormorant's baby brother—he is beautiful.

APRIL 7TH

Dick Starks came roaring up in his truck this morning early because his mother-in-law, Mrs. Breeden had fallen and wasn't making any sense. Jack was in the middle of his shower, but he went running over as quickly as he could get dressed. Mrs. Breeden was the lady who called Jack in the middle of the night a few years back because her husband had a bleeding ulcer and was stretched out on the back porch where he had fallen. Jack took care of him and was waiting with Mrs. Breeden for the ambulance to come. She was crying and she looked up at him with tears in her eyes and a voice that was quivering and said, "Dr. Fisher, my century plant is blooming out on the front porch. Would you like to see it?" Jack allowed as how he would, and they were out there looking at the beautiful blooms when the ambulance arrived.

APRIL 20TH

The headlines on the sports page today were that the Cormorant has been scratched from the list of Derby hopefuls. This was to be Ben's big break-through in racing. We are sick about it.

MAY 8TH

Another era in our lives ended today as a man came from Harrodsburg and bought the old boat. We had just stopped going to the river because of swim meets, so it was a good decision but very sad.

Even in leaving us, the old "Tiger" boat had the last laugh. As I was taking Mama back to Louisville, I realized that I hadn't thought to give the man the keys to the boat ignition. I called him when I got back to Midway to tell him that Jack and I would run them over after supper. That great old boat was a comedy of errors from the first day until the last. I was amazed at how very sad we were to see it hauled out of the driveway.

MAY 22ND

Jack went to the hospital last night at eleven-thirty to deliver a patient of Bob's, a thirteen-year-old girl who was terrified at the thought of having a baby. He didn't come home the rest of the night, and a phone call woke me up at five-thirty in the morning. A frantic man said that he had to have Jack come "right now" that "this girl has just had a baby in bed, and I need the doctor." I was immediately awake and gave him the number at the hospital. To try to calm him down, I told him that Jack couldn't be reached for any reason, to call me back and I would see what I could do. He hung up and then I was in a real swivet, scared to death that he would call back.

The man found Jack, thank God, and he came running over to Midway from the thirteen-year-old's delivery to take care of the home patient. This girl is from a nice family and the parents are fine people. The girl is not married but they are planning to keep the baby.

Yesterday, we watched the Preakness and Ben's Cormorant ran fourth to Seattle Slew, Iron Constitution, and Run Dusty, Run. He ran a great race at the start, then seemed to run out of steam. Ben and Ruth should be really pleased with his effort.

AUGUST 16TH

Lightning struck a barn on the Mitchell's farm where men were working in tobacco, and the nineteen-year-old Mitchell boy was killed outright. His dad was knocked down and temporarily paralyzed on one side. Jack had to go to the hospital to tell Mr. Mitchell about his son when he regained consciousness. It was a horrible tragedy.

AUGUST 16TH

Life is too short and too fragile. Elvis Presley is dead, and I am truly sad. I met him once backstage in 1955 when he came to perform at a country music show that my brother-in-law, Jim Bowling, had organized for the tobacco company that he worked for in New York City. Elvis was only twenty at the time, and had not yet burst on the national scene, but anyone who saw him and heard him sing had to recognize the fact that he had extraordinary talent. He was courteous and polite to me, calling me "Ma'am" even though I was just a couple of years older, but genuinely pleased because I had loved his music. Something about his manner sincerely touched me, and I have followed his career with awe ever since that night. Because of his incomparable talent, he had brought so much joy to so many people for so many years that I cannot believe he is gone. I feel as though a light has just gone out.

Bob Biddle told Ann Lewis that he has one month to make up his mind whether to stay here or to go to the next county with the unit that Ben had wanted to come here. I can't believe that he would want to leave us to go over there.

AUGUST 23RD

We drove Matt to Tampa University where he is starting on a marine biology degree. He is obsessed with the idea that this is what he wants to do with his life. So, we agreed to let him go as far away as Tampa. Can't imagine it will be Christmas before I see him again.

NOVEMBER 12TH

Woke up at two a.m. and Jack wasn't home. I lay awake until three-thirty when he came in. They had called him to the ER because there was a bad accident, then an OB had come in. He fell asleep as soon as he hit the bed, the lucky duck, because I was still wide-eyed when the alarm went off at 4:30 for me to take the kids to a swim meet.

DECEMBER 16TH

Jack came in at 5:45 this evening, and I had to tell him that Grady Hunter had died. She was eighty-four years old, and it broke his heart that he could not save her life. Her bed at Taylor Manor had been an extra-wide cot, and she had piled it so high with books and magazines that there was just a narrow space left for her ample body. A great lady and a good friend to Jack.

1978

The only thing we would need on a night like this is you.
—Catherine Riddle

JANUARY 17TH

We have fourteen inches of snow with four more due today. It is beautiful and dry—you can hardly make a snowball. Jack had a call at six this morning and he backed out of the garage into the driveway and the car is still stuck there. He has walked to the office to get their snow shovel to try to clear his way out. The temp is not bad, it was twenty-eight degrees in Lexington this morning.

Sunday, we picked up Jim Thomas and his wife to go to Jim Cogar's for supper. He fixed an apple drink that was a recipe of his great-grandfather's, and he poured a great slug of Scotch in the drink before realizing it wasn't Bourbon. Whereupon he grabbed the bottle of Bourbon and poured in another slug and handed it to us to drink. It was awful but we managed to get a taste down. He served wonderful chicken hash on a waffle for dinner—he is a gourmet cook.

While Jack and I were out shoveling the driveway this afternoon, Dick Starks walked up and insisted on helping us. Good friend.

JANUARY 18TH

Last night a lady called complaining of pleurisy pain and Jack met her at the office as his car wouldn't make it out her road. He was afraid it might be a coronary because she had been shoveling snow. So, he asked Bill Clark to take her to the hospital in his four-wheel drive vehicle. Bill was glad to oblige and just as the two of them walked into the hospital her heart arrested and they sent out a "Code 500" on her. Jack had to borrow the Riddles' truck to go tearing over, but she was dead before he arrived. Jack was sick about it—she was only fifty years old.

When Jack ran up to ask the Riddles for the use of their truck, she said, "Sure. The only thing we'd need on a night like this is you." Great people.

JANUARY 27TH

All the highways are blocked with snow around Midway today except for the Interstate, and the police are at every exit out there not allowing you to enter without chains. One hundred and fifty people were rescued nearby by helicopters—they had to leave their cars on the road where they stood.

The snow started two days ago when we went to the Chandler's in Versailles for supper. When we came out to come home, it looked like a blizzard was hitting. The roads were not slick yet, but the snow was heavy and blowing at such an angle that visibility was about eighteen inches.

Jack knows that road like the back of his hand so he could maneuver the thing.

Thursday must have set all kinds of records for Kentucky—the temperature went to just about two degrees all day but with fifty-mile an hour winds, the chill factor made it minus fifty-three. Jack walked up to the office to answer phones and to be available—we couldn't get our car out of the driveway. I walked up to the grocery by the post office as they were closing at ten-thirty a.m. because they had no bread, milk, eggs—or anything fresh—and no delivery trucks were coming through. Ann and Jim Bowling had to cancel their trip here as the New York airport told them that the Lexington and surrounding roads were all closed.

We have closed off Jenny's room, the living room and dining room in an effort to save fuel. We are playing Scabble with the kids in front of the fire in the den every night, and loving that. Thursday Jack called me to come and answer phones for him at the office because some people were beginning to get about. The feeling of dependency and closeness that this all brings about in the community is sort of nice.

JANUARY 29TH

We have had no mail deliveries since Wednesday—no milk trucks, and yesterday was the first day for bread trucks to get through. Our little grocery by the post office is still out of milk, cream, eggs, vegetables, and meat. I bought two boxes of crackers—we all love them toasted—and two boxes of oats (because we eat them mixed with salt and scalding water). Because of our Christmas turkey and ham, we are in good shape except for milk.

FEBRUARY 18TH

Jack jogged out the Weisenberger Mill Road one mile last night, first time on the roads since January 8th. The kids finally went back to school on Thursday. Our winter has set many records—I heard a man on the radio say that this winter there were more days when snow had continuously covered the ground than any other time since they started keeping records in 1872. Incredible.

JUNE 5TH

Went to a party given by the nurses for the surgeon and his wife. They are leaving Woodford Memorial Hospital to go to Maysville, Kentucky next week. They had planned food for one hundred people and only twenty-five showed up, which was too bad. Of the doctors, Jack and one other were there.

JUNE 7TH

It is pouring down rain this morning, but Jack ran his five mile jaunt anyway. He has started running really early in the mornings, four or five miles every other day, and that is working out so much better. It is helping him to keep his sanity.

We went by St. Joseph's hospital to see OB Wilder today. He is very thin and weak, hyperventilating, terrified, and has phlebitis again. A psychiatrist is looking in on him, and that scares him even more. He is in a bad way.

Jack delivered a baby this morning early—seems as if he doesn't deliver as many as he used to. The Big Three (Jack, Ben and Bob) are meeting with their advisor from Louisville tomorrow.

JUNE 11TH

The meeting is over and here are the results. Ben is going on half-time working only two days a week in the office or possibly four mornings, being on call half the time and drawing half salary. He said that three full days in a row just knocked him out and he was too exhausted to be on call. He said that he realized it was partly due to his active social life, but he loved that, and didn't want to give it up. This new schedule is to begin on July first.

JUNE 21ST

OB Wilder's wife wrote Jack a four-page letter on legal cap paper today talking about her husband's illness, and the closing paragraph was beautiful.

... and to you, Dr. Fisher, I express gratitude and appreciation from the bottom of my heart, for all your goodness, your understanding and care.

Not only are you OB's very excellent doctor, but you are his friend—his confidant—the one in whom he has the greatest trust and admiration.

JUNE 29TH

I worked at the office yesterday and it was grim. I am not very efficient and made some mistakes on the phone. One of the girls had to go to the hospital, and another is on vacation. I am going back to work today and I am really nervous about it. There is no way I can manage that front office alone when those phones start ringing.

JUNE 30TH

Yesterday at the office things were wild—a man with a heart attack, another man with a gunshot wound, and a lady with a fit or spasm—all worked in with the ordinary day's appointments every fifteen minutes. Not to be believed. Today only Bob will be in, so things should be better, please God.

JULY 11TH

Am sitting in the back yard anxiously waiting for Jack to come home. He is at the hospital seeing Phil House's daughter who dove in the shallow end of a neighbor's swimming pool and may have broken her neck. Mary Margaret, the girl's mother, had dashed to the office from Versailles with the girl, I'm sure she was too nervous to be driving well. Can't wait for Jack to come—am praying it is not as bad as it looked.

JULY 13TH

The House girl is going to be OK. What a horrible scare for everybody.

JULY 16TH

Jack had a patient die today. It is such a distressing thing for him. Something he never gets used to.

OCTOBER 29TH

Last Sunday we had a dinner party to celebrate Ben's sixtieth birthday. The guests were, Jim Cogar, Dick and Hilda Starks, Brerry and Libby Jones, my sister Ann and her Jim, Ben and Ruth.

The toast I wrote for him was:

Twenty years we've known him,
And he hasn't changed a hair.
He's just as sharp and handsome,
And he's twice as debonair.
He has kept his youthful figure—
But it really gives one pause
To think a man can reach this age,
And still believe in Santa Clause.

This was written with sincere apologies to Mr. Tom who originated the idea that Ben was the only man around who still believed in Santa Clause after he was forty years old.

NOVEMBER 30TH

Old Ella Wright died today and in spite of all my complaints, I'll miss her. I had really grown quite fond of her. Two weeks ago, she had convinced Jack that this time she was truly ill, and he had put her in Taylor Manor, so she did not die alone and scared as I had always feared she might.

Jack told me tonight that she reminded him of a Charles Dickens character—that she had little beady eyes and always wore a nightcap. She rubbed "Icy Hot" on herself continuously for her arthritis and the house positively reeked with the smell of it as she kept herself closed in with two vaporizers going full blast. She would be propped up in bed with her telephone and a little ringed pad where she wrote constantly about her illnesses. One of the specialists that she had seen had written a letter to Jack that her pains were rather diffuse, because they included not only her chest, but the abdomen, back, limbs, and, as she said herself, even her toe nails.

But she was a good sort and all she needed most of the time was a little attention. She never called for help whenever her grandchildren would be visiting, or when there were family get-togethers. She was happy anytime she was being noticed. She was seventy-nine years old. May she rest in peace.

DECEMBER 4TH

We went to a fancy dinner party at Ben and Ruth's and it was fun. We met an ex-Kentucky Governor there and he whispered in Jack's ear that he would see him on Friday. We wonder who in the world he thought Jack was as we had never seen him before in our lives. My dinner partner was Tony Benjamin, a delight.

1979

"This too shall pass."

—Ben Roach

MARCH 23RD

Interesting development. Jack just came home from lunch and informed me that a patient is suing him for $295,000 for malpractice. He brought home the man's medical chart and we looked at it together. All the while I felt like I was going to faint.

It seems that last year this patient was in to see Jack for some reason, and happened to mention a sore calloused hand. Jack probed it and the man asked him to open it. Jack suggested that he soak it instead, but the patient said it was really bothering him and wanted the place opened. Jack obliged him warning him to stay away from the stalls where he worked at the horse farm until the place was completely healed. Two days later, the place was really infected.

At this point Jack put him on an antibiotic, but two weeks later it was still bothering the man and Jack suggested that he go and see a surgeon about it. Jack got him a bed at Woodford Memorial, but he wanted to go to the University Hospital so Jack changed it for him—and that was the last thing Jack had heard about it. Until this.

My first reaction was intense fury, since I know how careful Jack is to do his very best for every single patient. He gives it all he's got every single time. I am absolutely sure that no malpractice was done and that the patient does not have a case. But you never can tell which way a jury will go. Our insurance goes to $300,000, so we are just under the wire.

MARCH 26TH

Have thought of nothing at all except the lawsuit. In the letter, it was claimed that Jack's instruments weren't sterile and that the man was given the wrong antibiotic. Both accusations are ludicrous. But at least Jack knows what kind of man he is dealing with. He always thinks the best of everyone, and just yesterday he was telling me the good things about this character. Every one of his "good points" I would add "And he is also a liar." Jack finally understood the gist of what I was saying.

I guess the worst result of the whole thing is that it has made me so bitter. I can't cope with the idea that someone would carelessly and utterly defame Jack when he has simply given his life in service to others. I utterly loathe the man and that is a hard thing to live with.

Incredibly sad weekend. OB Wilder died in the hospital Saturday morning. He had diabetes, a heart attack, and cancer of the lung. He was not in pain—he died very quietly and I guess it was a blessing. He was a very special friend to us.

Sunday was another cold, cloudy day and Jack and I spent most of it talking by the fire in the den. He was on call and busy from eight to four, the worst it had been for a long time. (I have visions of when the lawsuit appears in the papers that no one will call for a while, and I don't know whether I will be delighted or terrified.)

We went to the Funeral Home at five for OB, and he was dressed impeccably, as he always was in life. A really great man.

At ten-fifteen, Jack was called back to the hospital and I waited up for him. I've become more considerate of him during this episode and that is one good thing to come out of the mire.

MARCH 27TH

The distress of the lawsuit is ebbing. Time does not heal all pain. We have heard from various sources that the man suing came to do his duties at the horse stalls before his hand was healed. Thank God Jack has the record where he told that man that he simply must not do this because of the danger of infection. Surely this will help our case.

I spent the morning wiping each book on the bookshelves, washing the shelves, and putting the books back in some sort of order. Very therapeutic.

At two o-clock Jack and I went to OB's incredibly sad funeral. If ever a play had been written about Midway, he would have been one of the central characters. Maybe he would even have been the Greek Chorus.

MARCH 30TH

Last night Jack and I went to Ben and Ruth's for dinner with the entire office staff and it was wonderful to be with them. Ben has been very supportive of Jack over the lawsuit. His remark was, "This too, shall pass."

APRIL 8TH

After supper we walked over to Bridges Wilder's house. OB had wanted each member of our book club to have one of OB's beloved books when he died. I asked Jack to choose for us, and he took a small one on teaching psychology by William James that had obviously been read many times. It was underlined on almost every page, with many ideas written in the margins in his handwriting. A beautiful choice.

APRIL 9TH

Jack was called very late to a house here in Midway for a girl who was having a severe stomachache. When he arrived at the bedside it was obvious to him that the girl would deliver a baby momentarily right there in that bed. The grandmother kept pacing across the floor behind him muttering to herself. "There's gotta be some marryin' goin' on in this house." There were no complications and he was home fairly quickly.

APRIL 10TH

Jack received a letter yesterday from his company lawyer saying that they cover only $100,000 on our lawsuit, leaving us to cover the other $195,000. We do not understand that, as we had been told that our coverage went to $300,000. The lawyer wanted to know if Jack wanted to hire his own lawyer, since we "stood to lose so much." Jack still thinks justice will be done and right will prevail, so he wants to go with just this young company lawyer. I am beginning to believe there is no justice. I'm scared.

APRIL 17TH

Jack delivered a baby last night—was gone from one-thirty in the morning until five. Hard for him to get up at seven and go to work.

AUGUST 25TH

Heard yesterday that Alex had a coronary in D.C. and is in the hospital there. He is coming back to recuperate in a few weeks and we will know more then. He will be just thirty-eight years old on September seventeenth.

SEPTEMBER 15TH

The longest day of our lives. Alex has been flown back to the V.A. Hospital. He is to be under Russ McAllister's care. Russ called saying that they could not stop Alex's chest pain medically and were going on with all the tests and x-rays even though they do not like to do this while there is pain. He was very emotional on the phone and I know how bad things must be for Alex. I called Jack at the Woodford Hospital and he went up there right away.

Russ called later saying there was almost total blockage on the left side, and Alex was going into surgery for a triple by-pass at six p.m.. Jack wanted to stay with Alex's sister and her husband until it was all over. He didn't come home until one-forty-five—I had waited up for him and he ate a bowl of soup while we talked. The doctors said the operation was a complete success and Alex was doing well. Thank God.

OCTOBER 1ST

Alex is now at home at Woodburn recuperating. He looks loggy, but his marvelous sense of humor is intact. It is so great that he is alive and on the way to being well.

OCTOBER 12TH

Ben was down home last night, and he got to talking about old times again. He told about the home visit that he made in Versailles on the lady whose children were worried about her and asked him to look in on her. When he knocked on the door there was no answer, but he could hear noises inside. He cautiously pushed the door aside and called her name. When no answer came again, he made his way into the living room. He found her there, happy as a Lark, washing down the walls with a garden hose. Candles were lit positively all over the house. Quite a shock to say the least.

OCTOBER 23RD

Saturday night Emily and Bob Biddle had the entire office staff over for dinner. It was lovely. Ben told me that he had sold his best mare for enough money to pay for the Hick's farm in one fell swoop. It is obvious that Jack joined Ben in the wrong business.

NOVEMBER 28TH

Woke up at five-thirty a.m. with the phone ringing for Jack. I could not go back to sleep. I am worried about the office, as Jack told me last night that in the summer of 1981, Jim Roach and Ken Weaver want to come into the practice, with Henry

West coming six months later! Can't imagine spreading the patients that thin, but Jack is reluctant to be negative again. One good thing to come out of it would be the call schedule.

DECEMBER 7TH

Went to a great Christmas party at Ben and Ruth's and I wasn't dressed well enough. I was amazed at how much it bothered me.

DECEMBER 16TH

We went to a party last night at Wendell and Ann Harris' house with Pat and "B" Williams to celebrate the holidays. We have observed Christmas and each of our birthdays together since 1973, and the bonds of our friendship have grown strong throughout these years. Jack played a prank on Ann this year and we all thoroughly enjoyed it. Last year we gave her a present from Lehmans' and it was wrapped so beautifully that she exclaimed, "Oh, it is just too pretty to open. I'd rather have an empty box that came wrapped from Lehmans' than a present from anywhere else!"

Taking his cue from this remark, the other day Jack asked Miss Jeanette if he could pay her to wrap a small empty box and he told her why. She created an absolute master piece, so pleased at the compliment that she would not accept any pay for it. When Ann opened the package, she was a good sport about it being empty and we all had a good laugh.

All this reminded me of the time when Matt was about seven years old and he gave me a beautifully wrapped Christmas present obviously from Lehmans. When I opened it up, I was completely surprised to find a really inexpensive China rooster.

I knew this rooster would never have been sold at Lehmans. I cautiously asked Matt about it, not wanting to hurt his feelings. I asked where in the world he had found such a beautiful rooster.

"Oh, I bought the rooster at the drugstore," he told me. "But I took it to Miss Jeanette to wrap because she wraps better than they do." I did not have the heart to fuss at him, so I called Miss Jeanette to apologize for Matt's bothering her. She told me there was no reason to apologize—that she had been having a pretty bad day, and was so complimented by Matt's request that it had simply made her day and changed the way of that day for her. A very great lady.

DECEMBER 31ST

We had a meeting last Wednesday with Ben, Bob, Ken, Jimmy, and Henry (hail, hail, the gang's all here), as they are all interested in coming into the practice when they finish training. This scares me to death. They are all so very nice and I'm sure will be a credit to their profession wherever they practice, but I do not believe little old Midway can absorb it.

1980

JANUARY 5TH

I was rummaging through some drawers today and I came upon a letter that Miss Mayme wrote to me in December of 1969. We had taken the book, *A Christmas Memory* by Truman Capote to her as a birthday present and this was her beautiful thank you note:

> *Dear Mrs. Fisher,*
>
> *I certainly enjoyed to the fullest the "Christmas Memories." It brought to mind the old coal kitchen stove, and other things of that period*
>
> *No truer saying than that old folks "live in the past," and I am glad I can reminisce, for my days then as now have been happy. The subjects such as "Surely Goodness and Mercy" are so entertaining.*

> *My good wishes for the Christmas Season. The Children will make things joyous, and in your new home, makes for a happy time.*
> *My thanks and love,*
>
> *Miss Mayme*

She was well over ninety-years-old at that time, yet her positive approach to life had not dwindled in the least. A lovely lady.

JANUARY 9TH

There came in the mail today a letter from Jack's lawyers that the suit against him has been dropped. That the lawyers on the other side had decided that they did not have the grounds for a malpractice suit. Just like that. After all these months of worry and loss of sleep, Jack is notified that he is not going to stand trial for something he did not do. Will they be forced to print a retraction of the degrading notice that appeared in the local newspapers stating that he faced a malpractice lawsuit? I am told they will not. There was an enclosure in the notice that Jack was to sign stating in effect that he would not counter-sue, and I was so angry that I threw it into the fire as soon as Jack went back to the office after lunch. Let the old man and his lawyers sweat a little.

JANUARY 24TH

Thursday our advisor from Louisville arrived to talk about the practice. He said that taking in Jimmy, Henry and Ken just did not seem logical. He is not sure the community of Midway would have enough patients to go around. He suggested that the three new ones go together and build an office on the lot behind the present one and collect only from the patients they see. Jack is uncomfortable with all the discussions, he hates arguments and debates of any kind.

JANUARY 30TH

Miss Mayme is failing. Jack thinks she must have suffered a small stroke because she is seeing imaginary people and doesn't recognize anyone anymore. How sad. Guess everything is entitled to wear out after one-hundred and three years.

JANUARY 31ST

Yesterday the snow kept coming all day really fine and thick. There was about an accumulation of close to eight inches. I put on Peter's snow-suit and walked to the post office, Lehman's to see Miss Jeanette, and to the grocery there. I pulled home fourteen dollars-worth in that little grocery cart—hard to do in all that snow. Then I pushed the snow off the shrubs with a broom and shoveled the walk. It all needs doing again.

FEBRUARY 5TH

Jim Cogar called yesterday morning to say that Miss Mayme had died the night before. He sounded almost relieved, as I guess we all were. She had said that she was "ready to go to the Lord" for several years now. A wonderful lady with a totally upbeat attitude every day of her long life. She told me several years ago that she worried about young people these days as they seemed so easily bored. She said she could honestly say she had never been bored a single day in her life. I believed her.

FEBRUARY 13TH

Ben came down last night and he and Jack talked about possibilities at the office. He is going to see his son Jimmy at the end of the month, and wanted to know what to tell him. Jack had to drag his feet at taking in three partners almost at once, and Ben was great as he always is in time of crisis. They are both very excited at the prospect of practicing with Jimmy, as he seems to have all the right qualities for "The Practice".

MARCH 13TH

About the practice: Jack is working harder than ever, with Ben in the office half time, and Bob Biddle making noises that he might be quitting as of July 1st. Jimmy is due to start the following July 1st and Ken Weaver and Henry West have been put on hold. Everyone pretty much agrees that Midway is just not big enough for that kind of clinic. We are waiting for the dust to settle.

APRIL 14TH

Bob is quitting as of July 1st. I do wish he would stay one more year as that is when Jimmy is coming. I dread the year for Jack although Ben has agreed to practice full time for the interim year.

JULY 4TH

Mrs. Roach, Ben's mother, died on Wednesday at Taylor Manor, and was buried on Saturday. They had the service on the farm—all the children were there plus most of the grandchildren and many great-grandchildren. Jack felt highly honored to be named pall bearer along with her grandsons and Don Johnson, the man who had worked for the Roaches most of his life.

Mrs. Roach was so very kind to us when we moved here. She was always crazy about Jack. She played the piano beautifully, loved good music, the Opera and Cincinnati. Mr. Tom said that she thought you'd have to go through Cincinnati to get to Heaven. She was buried in Lexington beside Tom.

OCTOBER 11TH

We went to the wedding of Betty Wherle and Whit Biggerstaff today in the Versailles Baptist Church. Betty has worked in the office for years, and she is a wonderful girl. Her first husband died an untimely death with a brain tumor after much pain and suffering for the entire family. The wedding was beautiful—with her children and the children of her new husband all taking part in the ceremony. Her first in-laws were there on the front pew of the church giving her their blessing, and it was a very joyful occasion.

OCTOBER 14TH

On Thursday, Old Jesse's house in Midway caught fire and he got out with his dog but he ran back in—to get his money as we all suppose as he did not believe in banks. He did not get back out and it was all so very sad. Our neighbor, Betty Bright took the little dog to take care of—she is naming it "Jesse" as no one knew Its name. Poor old Jesse—what a way to die.

OCTOBER 30TH

I am in a state of shock. Yesterday, I went for my yearly checkup with my gynecologist and he found a lump on the far side of my left breast. I have felt numb and teary ever since. He suggested that I contact a general surgeon and get his opinion.

I came staggering home—Jack was putting in the storm windows, and I told him about it and started crying. He was so great to me, and when I told him I was terrified at the prospect of having cancer, he put his arm around me tight, looked at me wide-eyed and desperate and declared, "Join the human race— we are all scared. What makes you think you're any different?"

It was vintage Jack Fisher and exactly what I needed. He was right of course. And then I was able to sort of get ahold of myself and to consider my options.

NOVEMBER 22ND

Almost a month has passed since I last wrote in this journal. I did have to have surgery as the diagnosis was "cancer" and it has taken a while to get used to the idea. Dr. Chuck Mooney did the modified mastectomy—it did not involve any arm muscles, so I am very lucky. All the tests for spread were negative, so just maybe I'll have a few more years. I haven't been so depressed since the evaluation as that wouldn't change anything. I keep thinking I have been blessed all my life with such an abundance of good things that I was overdue a mishap. Seems as though I've got one.

Our friends have been more than supportive—I've written eighty-two thank you notes for food and flowers. I have received sixty-three notes from Jack's patients who I didn't even know. From that viewpoint the entire ordeal has been beautiful.

DECEMBER 2ND

Had a talk with Dr. Mooney, my surgeon, and he told me that for every ten ladies that he operates on like me, with the same prognosis, eight are cured and two have recurrence. It gives me reason to be cautiously optimistic, but he repeated to me that somebody has to be the two, and I should be careful. I keep praying that God will help me cope with whatever happens to me—I can't bring myself to ask Him not to send adversity as I have had it so easy all my life—until now. Chuck Mooney has become very important to me as an ally.

DECEMBER 15TH

Drove to swimming tonight and asked Jack to pick up fried chicken and slaw for supper. He appeared with one half-pint of slaw and nine pieces of chicken—for FIVE people! He is so funny—glad he is not spacey where his patients are concerned! We all went to bed a little hungry.

DECEMBER 18TH

This will be an especially meaningful Christmas for us this year. The Good Lord let us know that we can't take time for granted, and we are just grateful that we will all be here together for Christmas 1980.

DECEMBER 30TH

Went to Lexington with Bett Weisenberger and Hilda Starks to celebrate Hilda's birthday. Special friendships have taken on a new meaning for me in the past two months, and these two are what you'd call special. We have been friends since 1959 and they have never disappointed me in any way. We had a good day.

1981

*I sat there in severe back pain while Dr. Roach took a nap. Is
that fair?*

—Angry Patient

NEW YEARS DAY

Jack was at the hospital all day long—in the throes of a
flu epidemic and he is going night and day. I slept an hour in
front of the fire in the den and then took down all the Christmas
decorations. Good day.

FEBRUARY 6TH

Yesterday was a very special day for us—Matt received his
acceptance to dental school at University of Kentucky. They
sent a beautiful letter and we called him at Tampa with the good
news. He was elated—kept saying that he couldn't believe it.

FEBRUARY 18TH

Jack came in around nine tonight—he had been up talking with our good friends Jean and Ike Rouse for a long time. Jean had come to see him two weeks ago with a low back ache. He sent her to a specialist and it was determined that she had cancer spread from her malignant breast tumor that he had removed eight years ago. She is now going to Lexington for radiation. The doctor was afraid it had spread to the liver, but all tests were negative there. The lesions are on the spine and cannot be removed. I am heartsick.

FEBRUARY 19TH

Jack was distressed tonight as two Versailles doctors have called a meeting to try to remove the administrator at the hospital. They don't want a health center that has already been approved for the hospital to the tune of five point one million dollars and it is already half built. Jack doesn't see any way around it at this time.

FEBRUARY 25TH

I quilted until Jack came home at eleven tonight from another meeting concerning the hospital. It is trying times over there now.

MARCH 1ST

We are going to John Willie McDaniel's funeral in a minute. He was our only police force when we came here in 1959, and he often rode on horseback. There was virtually no crime of violence in Midway as everyone was scared to death of John

Willie. They told us of the time that the Versailles police threw some hoodlums out of their town only to see them turn down the road that led to Midway. The police called John Willie to tell him that trouble was on the way. He drove out to the public school and parked his car sideways across the road where they would have to pass. He leaned across the car and crossed his arms over his chest. As the renegades came tearing down the Pike, they spotted him waiting for them. They slammed on their brakes and veered into Bill Buster's gate to turn around. They did not crave a confrontation with John Willie.

He was a friend to me from the very first day. He let me ride his horse one time and that animal headed for the barn. He was rearing up several times with me screaming on its back. I managed to slide off and not let go of the reins, so I could lead him back to the fence where Jenny and Matt were hanging terrified, and John Willie was bent double laughing. I'll miss him.

He had been our law enforcement officer for thirty-five years, and we will never be able to replace him.

MARCH 24TH

Jack has been wonderful to me this past week. My arm is swelling as a result of the surgery, and I have a nagging low backache which makes me fear the worst. He is constantly reassuring me, and never loses patience with my agitation. A most remarkable man.

APRIL 20TH

Easter Sunday has come and gone, and it was a good one. It was rainy and cold all day and we even had a fire in the fireplace. Peter, Ann T, Jack and I went to Mass at eight, and came back to the usual Easter breakfast at Coemma's church. It consists of bacon (or sausage), grits, eggs, biscuits, coffee or tea, and orange juice. It is always delicious. Old Mr. Hamilton was there once again, and he played, "Easter Parade" on the piano for Jack and we all sang.

He played with a musical group when he was young—he must be ninety-years-old—and he is still a superb pianist.

At ten Peter and Ann T took off for Louisville for the family gathering, and we were nervous about Peter driving it for the first time without us. Jack was on call so the two of us stayed home and I answered the phone for him.

MAY 1ST

Through the years Jack and Ben have gotten many, many letters thanking them for their special concern, or praising their ability to heal. Today Ben got a letter of a different nature, and we are teasing the life out of him. It went:

To: Dr. Roach
Subject: Office visit April 22nd, 1981. I was not pleased with the way I was treated on the above date.
Betty did not take my temperature. No one told me my pulse rate.
No one told me my blood pressure. No one told me the results of the
Urine analysis. In addition, I sat there in severe back pain while
Dr. Roach took a nap. Is that fair?
Respectfully,

Then she signed the letter and enclosed a check for what the visit charged.

This letter is particularly funny because every now and then, Ben has been seen running out of an examining room in the middle of listening to a long-winded patient and splashing cold water on his face several times before going back into the arena. He will never live this down.

JULY 1ST

Jim Roach is to start in at the office this week and he is direly needed. He is very serious and conscientious and extremely intelligent. I really think he will fill the bill. After he is orientated, Ben plans to drop back to half time.

JULY 15TH

I am beginning to understand some of the frustrations that people are feeling with medicine. Jack was seeing one of Bob's patients and determined that the daughter needed surgery. He scheduled it with a Woodford Hospital surgeon and a Frankfort obstetrician. When both doctors had arrived at the hospital, the parents decided they wanted to take her to Lexington where their favorite surgeon would do the job.

Jack called their favorite in Lexington to try to set this up with him, but he said another surgeon was covering for him. Jack called this man who became livid and said he had not been asked to cover! And indeed he would not. He told Jack that one of them would call him back. Jack sat cooling his heels for quite a while, then the first one called saying he would not accept the patient, that Jack should get the first two that had been asked and have it done at Woodford. But both of these doctors had gone back home by this time. In utter frustration Jack called on a surgeon friend, only to find out he was vacationing in Colorado. He next called the surgeon who was covering for his friend, who miraculously said to send the patient on up now. The episode had taken Jack more than three hours. It turned out to be a frustrating way to spend a Saturday afternoon.

SEPTEMBER 5

Every day when Matt comes home from dental school, he hits the back door screaming, "Migraine! Migraine!"—grabs two aspirin and collapses on the couch until supper.

I had a horrible headache last night at suppertime and had thrown together a vat of vegetable soup and very little else, even though I know the children can barely tolerate vegetable soup. I was at the stove stirring up the caldron, when Matt, Peter and Ann T came in to the table, picked up their big bowls, cupping them with both hands, and formed a line to the stove. Then in absolute unison with great, long, sad faces, they sang the marvelous opening lines of the play "Oliver!" In which the children complain about the fact that all they ever get to eat is gruel. It was beautifully timed, and we all simply cracked up. Miraculously the headache went away.

SEPTEMBER 17

Bob Biddle came driving up in an enormous trail mobile that he had bought to drive to Utah with his family. It was great fun to see him. We all sat in the trail mobile and talked until time for supper.

OCTOBER 13

Jack had a meeting at the office with Ben, Jim, and Ken Weaver, and the upshot is that they told Ken that the office could not absorb another man this year. I am sorry because Jack really likes Ken, but I think they made the right decision.

The gossip is all over town that some men are interested in building a subdivision across from the Girl's College, with condominiums and townhouses in it. High-rise comes to Midway. Say it isn't so.

OCTOBER 20TH

Went to the library to look up a newspaper article that had been written about all of Ruth's contributions to the community, as a serious man wants to nominate Ben and Ruth to be the co-recipients of the award at the Annual Brotherhood Awards Banquet of the Bluegrass Chapter of the National Conference of Christians and Jews. It will be given next March. I found the article, copied it verbatim, and sent it on to the man.

NOVEMBER 10TH

Bruce Davis called Jack a week ago and said he was spitting up blood. Jack put him in the hospital where he found that Bruce has cirrhosis of the liver, hepatitis and swelling of the brain. On Friday Jack told me that Bruce has a fifty-fifty chance of making it. I have been in abject despair ever since.

When we came to Midway, he was delightful, funny, generous, and full of love for his fellow man. I loved to hear him tell the stories of the men who worked for him. I remember him telling about the time he went into one of their homes early one morning and there was a bowl of gravy in the center of the table, with a spoon standing straight up the middle of it. He really cared about these people, and I loved his stories.

Then came the heart attack, the following problem with alcohol, and the downward drift into bad health. I wish I had kept in closer contact with him—he has always been such a "human" person—and I still consider him the best friend I ever had. He accepted my shortcomings, and never once expected me to be better than I am.

Jack is sending Bruce on up to the V.A. Hospital because of the probability of a lengthy stay.

NOVEMBER 24

On Friday the weirdest thing happened to Honeywood Rouse. She came tearing into the office, very gray-faced and wild-eyed, saying that her neighbor, Ann Piper, her grandchild, and her daughter-in-law, Jean, were all sitting straight up in chairs with their eyes wide open, but they were dead.

Jack and his nurse dashed out to Ann Piper's house, afraid there had been a gas leak. Ann met them at the door dressed in her hat and coat, clearly OK. Jack went back to the office to check Honeywood who had no previous mental problems, but she had driven off soon after he had gone to Ann's. He knew he had to find her, but pulled her chart before he went looking. There on the chart, he saw where Ben had placed one of those little discs behind her ear to relieve her dizziness and one of the side effects may be hallucinations. So, instead of having to deal with a stroke as he had feared, he ran down and removed the disc. Several hours later, she was back to normal, although badly shaken. So were the office girls and Jack as she had been thoroughly convincing.

DECEMBER 5

Jack, Jenny, and I had a ball last night at the hospital staff dance that was held at St. Leo's gym. Jenny was invited because she is now working at the office. We enjoyed sitting with the Biddles—Bob has always been one of Jenny's favorites.

DECEMBER 27

We came home from the family get-together on Christmas Day in Louisville by six-thirty to cover the practice, because Ben and his entire family go to a movie on Christmas night every year. This custom started long ago when he was in practice by himself, and it was a place to hide on this special night to be with his family where patients couldn't bother him.

Jack and I rode out to see Bruce Davis who has been dismissed from the V.A. Hospital. Bruce has made the first hurdle, and we are cautiously optimistic.

1982

Life is so daily.
—Robina

JANUARY 1

Jack came in from the hospital around eleven-thirty last night and he, Matt, Ann T and I celebrated the end of old 1981. We walked down the street ringing the iron triangle and someone was shooting off firecrackers. We put the stereo speakers on the terrace and played "Auld Lang Syne" as loud as it would go—twice. The phone rang and it was Roberta House who lives about two blocks away, thanking us for the wonderful music. She meant it. To bed at one o'clock.

JANUARY 11

Ben went to see a patient who has been running a fever of one hundred five degrees for a couple of days, with either flu or hepatitis and Ben drew blood for some tests. Just as he put the needle back into his bag to throw away, he accidently stuck it into his own hand thus practically inoculating himself with whatever the man has. Flu would be bad enough, but hepatitis B can be deadly. Some years ago, a doctor in Versailles did the very same thing and died at age forty-five by contracting hepatitis B from the prick. Ben was wild—ran to the hospital immediately to take a huge dose of gamma globulin. We are holding our breaths awaiting the outcome of the tests.

JANUARY 14

The feverish patient tested negative for hepatitis. Thank God!

JANUARY 27

Talked to Ruth a long time on the phone. While we were out of town last week, Ben turned onto an icy Midway Road coming from Versailles. He spun around totally out of control, and slammed through a plank fence, barely missing two trees. The car was demolished—Ben was not even bruised. He continues to be the luckiest man alive.

There was a time in Ben's life shortly after we came here when he drove terribly fast over these narrow roads, and he had three really bad accidents in a very short time—and he was not hurt in any of the three. I remember the details of one of these wrecks. He was coming home from Lexington down US 421, and an old man pulled out right in front of him. Slamming his brakes on and swerving, he was nevertheless unable to miss the old fellow and the two cars rammed together. Ben was not hurt but his car was demolished. He jumped out and ran over to see what had happened to the old man and was appalled to see his face all mottled and turning blue. Ben instinctively ran his fingers down into the man's throat to see what was causing the blockage and he felt something that did not belong there. He pulled on it and out came a huge wad of tobacco—whereupon the old man coughed, started breathing again, and came around.

FEBRUARY 9

Jack had to make a home visit at a grandmother's house because she called hysterical saying her grandson was in a coma. When Jack tore down, the sheriff was there and it was apparent that it was not a coma, but a drug reaction. The sheriff and their men held the boy down so Jack could give him a shot but that did not faze him. They took him to the University Hospital, who wouldn't keep him, so now he is in Woodford Hospital. We all feel so sorry for the grandmother.

FEBRUARY 20

Twenty-three years ago today Matt was born at nine o'clock in the morning at Norton Infirmary in Louisville. He was a large baby—eight pounds, nine ounces, and great looking.

At that time Jack was tearing to one hospital to visit his Dad who was dying of cancer, over to the next one to see Matt and me, plus carrying on his schedule of "on duty" thirty-six hours at Louisville General with twelve hours "off."

We were all subdued over our happiness with Matt because of our utter despair over Mr. Fisher. Mr. Fisher died the day Matt was five weeks old—on Good Friday—a most remarkable, wonderful man. I could not have loved him more had he been my own father. He was fifty-two years old—we were devastated.

MARCH 11

The dinner was last night to honor Ben and Ruth as the co-recipients of the coveted award for outstanding service, given by the Bluegrass Chapter of the National Conference of Christians and Jews. It was quite an honor for them. Ben had us sitting at the table with his family right near the speaker's table.

MARCH 13

Jack called all the young doctors who have come to Woodford Memorial since it became a Family Health Care Center and asked them to come for supper on March twenty-fourth and they all accepted. It will be a lot more than twelve people so we will have to put up another table in the dining room. We were delighted that they were all able to come. Can't believe the staff at Woodford Memorial has increased by so many.

MARCH 18

Jack and I walked up to Ben and Ruth's farm with Tom Bombadil, and they were both out walking with their son Tommy. It was a very special day as spring was in the air. This time of year really does seem extraordinary as you grow older. It is the beginning over again—much more than the start of the calendar year. You thank God for all the times you've seen it—felt it—and realize how short it all has been. Too few springs when you count them up. Jim Cogar's hill is positively bursting with buttercups.

APRIL 1

Yesterday afternoon, Jack and I went to a memorial service for old Ivan Davis who had died on March twenty-eighth at the age of eighty-one. When we first came to Midway and lived in the little gray house, Ivan would appear early every Saturday morning—reeking with the smell of bourbon—selling eggs and wanting Jenny to ride with him in the truck to make his other deliveries. Week after week, I'd come up with another flimsy excuse because I didn't want to hurt his feelings, but I wasn't about to let Jen get into a truck smelling of bourbon! A few years later, he and his wife Katherine—both admitted alcoholics—stopped drinking cold turkey and never had another drink to my knowledge.

They lived in an enormous old brick house on a beautiful farm off of Old Frankfort Pike about a mile east of Nugent Crossroads. When Ivan and Katherine stopped drinking, he started a huge vegetable garden to one side of the house. He brought baskets full of fresh vegetables in to people he liked who lived in town. He particularly liked to bring zucchini, and I remember the morning I saw him drive up in his truck, loaded down with zucchini—and I had to run out to the breezeway to stash away the batch he had brought two days before that I had not used yet. He was so great to want to share, and I didn't want to hurt him.

They had to let the big old house go—Katherine was ill and they moved to Florida. She died a short time later and he returned to live in Woodford County in a little house in Versailles. He settled down and started once again making his rounds to visit his friends. He seemed very lonely. About a month ago he came to Jack with a chest cold and Jack ordered a chest x-ray. There was a huge tumor on his lung, and he started going rapidly down. Because of his age there was no thought of surgery—they were considering chemotherapy when he died.

After a service in the tiny Presbyterian church, we all went to a buffet at Graham and Maryann's and told our personal stories about Ivan. He would have approved.

APRIL 19

Ben has decided to work full days just on Wednesdays and Thursdays and half days on Mondays and Tuesdays. Jimmy will get twenty-five percent of the income from the practice, plus a little more percentage since his dad dropped back. Jack will get about forty percent all told plus rent from Jimmy for his (Jack's) half of the building and equipment. Ben wants to forgo all of Jimmy's payments to him—he is a very generous father. And we are off to another year.

APRIL 30

In the middle of the night last night, Jack went to the Craig's house to make a home visit. The house was dark when he arrived at the door, and he knocked loudly before he was able to rouse anybody. Finally, a light came on and Jack could see Ida Lee coming to the door struggling to get her robe on. She opened the door with a dazed look on her face and asked, "What in the world has happened, Dr. Fisher?"

"What do you mean 'what has happened', Ida Lee?" Jack asked back. "I am here because you called for me to come to see about Marshall."

"I did not!" she exclaimed laughing. "Dr. Fisher, we were both sound asleep until you woke us up a minute ago! You have had a bad dream!"

He stared at her unbelievingly and then realized that she was probably right. He sat in the car a minute trying to figure out if someone else had called and he had just mixed up the names, or if truly he had dreamed the whole thing. He came home and went back to bed, half expecting a call from an irate patient demanding to know what was keeping him, but the call never came.

MAY 12

Had a dinner party last night for Jim Cogar with his good friend from Baltimore and Jim Thomas with his friend, Becca Lewis. Jim C. was telling some of the remarks that his wonderful help (Robina) in Williamsburg had made and a few of them are worth recording.

"Life is so daily." (Self-explanatory).

"She's risin' 'bove her raisin'." (Said when a girl married socially "up".)

And my favorite, "Dust don't interest me." This was said by Robina when Jim had come home late from a lecture that he was giving, and he was expecting dinner guests momentarily. He walked into the kitchen and was gratified by the wonderful aroma of Robina's cooking. But when he went on into the hall it was obvious that the house had not been touched with a dust rag. Startled, he ran back into the kitchen and exclaimed, "Robina! You haven't cleaned the house! And the guests are due to arrive any minute!"

She kept on stirring the soup and she quietly replied, "I know, Mr. Cogar. But dust don't interest me." Jim grabbed a rag and wildly began dusting the furniture.

MAY 13

Jack had an OB to go into the hospital who isn't due until June twenty-fourth. She is very small, and he fears the baby will be tiny. He stayed with her all night, and she still has not delivered. He came home a minute ago to try to get a little sleep.

MAY 16

A man came into the office Friday saying he had recently moved here from Texas and that he had narcolepsy. That he was taking seventy-five mgs Preludin twice a day for it. That he had been worked up at the University of Houston. Jack set him up with an appointment with a neurologist in three days and gave him enough medicine to last for the interim.

The man went to the neurologist straight away and was waiting to be seen when he overheard the nurse calling Jack for some more information. He told the nurse that he had to leave for a minute to pick up his wife, and, of course, never came back. Jack had been taken—the poor man must have been an addict.

JUNE 15

Jack brought home a sheet put out by the hospital last night showing the number of patients each of the doctors on the staff have hospitalized between January first and June first. My husband led the pack with one hundred fifty-three.

JULY 4

We went to a small, intimate gathering of good friends at the Hicks' pool to celebrate the holiday. Bruce Davis was there drinking two large Coca-Colas, saying that he was not as much fun as he used to be. Not a human being there agreed.

AUGUST 23

Am waiting for Jack to come home. Alex is back in the hospital with heart trouble. Two of the three veins that were bypassed have some blockage again. There is no involvement in the third. There is some obstruction in the lower right quadrant, which was not involved in 1979, but it is too low to operate.

We took Peter to Indiana University yesterday, and I am incredibly sad. He is our most vulnerable child—and I pray God will help him to have a good four years and help him to keep a healthy mind and body—to say nothing of his soul.

AUGUST 24

Alex's surgery is scheduled for next week at St. Joseph's. It will be a quadruple bypass, if not five. He is in good spirits, pleased that they found the trouble before he had an actual heart attack. It is still a grim prospect to be facing again after only three years.

AUGUST 31

The surgery was yesterday, and it turned out that Alex had to have a quadruple bypass. We went to the hospital last night and the doctors said that his vessels were in better shape than they had dared to hope. And it had been a good operation. Thank God.

SEPTEMBER 2

We visited Alex but I waited in the hall as he was still in CCU. Jack knocked on the door and when a little nurse answered it, Jack said, "Dr. Fisher to see Dr. Alexander." She said she would check.

She came back in just a second with a grin on her face and said, "Dr. Alexander said you'd have to give the password." We knew then that he was feeling his oats.

SEPTEMBER 11

We went to Lexington to a fun party at the Biddles'. It was outside in the yard, and they had music and way too much to eat and drink. He is no longer with the medical group in the next county but is now doing emergency room service in one of the Lexington hospitals. Super guy. We are always sorry he left the practice.

NOVEMBER 22

Barb Moraja and I have our appointments with our surgeon, Chuck Mooney. I guess we will be nervous for the rest of our lives when going to a doctor. That fear goes with the disease, Dr. Mooney told us. The "Big C" is a formidable foe. Didn't sleep well last night.

NOVEMBER 25

Thanksgiving Day, my twenty-seventh with Jack. Our first was in 1955 the year before we married, when he went with Daddy and me to visit Grandmother Jones in Lyon County for the four days. We went in our old green Chevy and, as Daddy and I hated to drive with the heater on, we just wore heavy coats. Jack told me later that he absolutely froze to death the entire five hours both ways, even though he was wearing layers of heavy clothes.

On that Thanksgiving afternoon, my cousins took Jack on a turkey shoot, and he was frantic that he might accidently hit one. He came close but missed. My cousins liked him on the spot and that pleased me to no end. They are not an easy bunch to move into, but, once you are in, you are in for life.

Monday at the doctor's was a great day for Barb and me as we had clear sailing and are to come back in another six months. We both are to have mammograms before we see him again in May. I love Barb—we have a lot in common now, united by the "Big C."

DECEMBER 7

This would have been Daddy's eighty-sixth birthday had he not died almost fourteen years ago. Also, it is the well-remembered anniversary of the attack on Pearl Harbor. I recall that day distinctly. We lived out on a farm in Lyon County that was without running water, electricity, or telephones. We had a big floor model Philco radio, and the family would sit around it and listen for hours at night.

We had celebrated Daddy's birthday that day, and had the radio on, waiting for Jack Benny's show to start. They interrupted the regular programming to break the news of the attack, and Daddy became terribly upset. Ann and I were giggling and laughing having no idea of the consequences of that news bulletin. He shouted at us to get quiet so he could hear—one of the very few times in our lives that he ever really raised his voice at us. Forty-four years ago—a lifetime.

1983

The ox is in the ditch.

—Bill Bridgeforth

JANUARY 2

Christmas was wonderful because we were all together. Matt slept in the basement, Peter on the den couch because Mama was here and sleeping in his bed. Jenny and Ann T were in their beds and every space was filled. We had our Christmas Eve dinner after we went to Mass, and this year Ann T read the scripture from Luke.

Christmas Day was spent in Louisville with all of Jack's family, and it was a very special time for us. We were home by six o'clock. Around eleven-thirty the Versailles Police called saying they needed Jack to come to calm down one of his young patients. The boy had been arrested for driving under the influence of alcohol, had resisted arrest and was totally out of control. I rode over with Jack as we both felt like we had to go. I was sitting in a locked car in front of the county jail when the clock in the courthouse struck midnight of Christmas Day. One of the officers on duty came out to the car to wish me a Happy New Year.

JANUARY 27

Had to take Ann T to school again today as Jack was delivering another baby. He was up at two-thirty a.m. on Wednesday for a delivery and four-thirty this morning. He is getting too old for those hours!

Saturday Jack was busy all morning long—then he went to the funeral of a favorite patient of his and was a pallbearer. This patient was a fifty-one year old man who was recovering nicely from a heart attack but had a stroke and died. Really too bad.

We went to dinner at Kenney Harper's along with Jeanette Lehman and her brother Joe, and Jim Cogar. It was to celebrate Jim's seventy-seventh birthday and we felt very privileged to be included as the others had been friends for nearly seventy years.

FEBRUARY 23

Yesterday Jack was on the phone forty-five minutes to a visiting Frenchman and his wife, trying to persuade the man to go to St. Joseph's Hospital for a work-up as Jack thinks he has histoplasmosis. All the man would accept was for Jack to come and "give me a shot".

Jack had tried several drugs on him without results and he was running a one hundred and three degree temperature today.

The wife accused Jack of wanting to put him in the hospital for the wrong reasons, but the husband got on the phone and agreed to meet him at eight o'clock the next morning. Jack called Russ McAllister to set up the appointment.

At seven forty-five this morning the wife called to say that they had found another doctor who was willing to come out and give the shot, no questions asked. Jack would have to call and cancel them out. Frustrating affair in more ways than one.

MARCH 3

I went to the office to answer the phones for them today— the first time in a long time. When Bill Bridgeforth came to the desk window and saw me there by myself, he said, "Well, well. The ox is in the ditch." Absolutely true.

MARCH 13

Finished reading "The Iceman Cometh" by Eugene O'Neill, and it was all about pipe dreams and the end of pipe dreams. It gave me a queasy feeling that my age-old dream of writing a book about Jack's life as a country doctor is just a pipe dream. That I put off doing any actual work on it, yet I tell everyone in hearing distance that I am ready to begin it. The truth may be that I'm scared to death to start. It has been my greatest hope of doing something meaningful with my mind—and the fear of not being able to bring it off may boggle every effort to start. Eugene O'Neill isn't easy to live with.

MARCH 31

Sunday while Jack was jogging out a country road, he was bitten severely by a family's German shepherd in the calf of his leg. Jack phoned that family when he came home and the dogs have had their shots. Thank God.

The woman said to him, "They are not bad dogs. Why don't you come out and I will introduce you to them." She left herself wide open for a wonderful retort, but Jack wouldn't say anything.

MAY 5

Due to different hours and different priorities, Jack, Ben, and Jimmy have decided that their income shall equal the percentage of patients they actually see. The three of them met with lawyer friend Joe Arnold this morning to set it up.

MAY 12

We were trying to get off last night to go to Louisville as Ben won the award as Kentucky's Outstanding Family Practitioner of the Year. At five o-clock, Jack was at the hospital working with an OB who had become totally hysterical, screaming, and hollering, and finally passing out in the chair.

About that time back in Midway, Bill McDonald (the Christian church minister), appeared at our door with a fifth grade boy who had gotten beaned on the head with a baseball and his eye was enormously swollen. I packed ice on it and called Jack to wait at the hospital until Bill could get the boy there. The peculiar thing that worried Bill and me about the eye was that the pupil was smaller than the other eye rather than larger as you would expect.

So, Jack and I were very late arriving at the dinner but we were there in time for the presentation of the award. The master of ceremonies listed all of Ben's wonderful contributions to the medical field, and it was gratifying to hear him receive public acclaim for his incredible service. Ben, in his acceptance speech, said, "The only way I was free to do all the things that gave me this award tonight was that I had a partner, Dr. Norman 'Norm' Fisher, who was at home taking care of my practice for me."

Vintage Ben Roach.

JULY 2

Jack brought home a letter tonight that he had received from an old patient who had moved away some time ago. It read:

Dear Pal of long ago,

I so often think of you and the nurses that was so good to give me samples. Don't get any now. I think I must write, but put it off. Hope all are well wonder how Dr. Roach is. After John sold the place and broke the Will I had to move. I was to get half of everything. I got 1/3 wouldn't got 1/3 if I hadn't got a lawyer. Hard on me to pack and move.

My son passed away in May. My only sister passed away last March. 3 deaths in a year almost more than I can stand. Took me to the emergency at funeral. Passed out when I saw my son. Cancer was all over his body. In my family only me and my sister, now she is gone. Only me left. No husband. No children. Sure is hard on me to be alone. I'm old. New neighbors, new church. If I was younger wouldn't be so bad to make new friends. They're good at the church to visit and pray. I work in a store day or two a week where food and clothes is given to the poor. It's charity work better than looking at the 4 walls.

My son's Hospital bill for 3 weeks 30 thousand dollars. 2 more weeks 20 thousand. Terrible to be sick, don't have a good doctor in this town, got one not very good, only got a flu shot from him, he dockered my sister. I miss all the nurses and my quiet easy Doctor. God bless all.

It was signed with love. Letters like that can break your heart.

SEPTEMBER 3

The phone rang at daybreak today and when Jack answered, a lady began, "Dr. Fisher, my daughter has lost her mind. She has locked herself in the house—please get over here and do something." He went right away not sure of just exactly what she thought he could do.

SEPTEMBER 4

Jack left here early this morning to meet the police and the mother at the county jail to help the daughter. When he got there yesterday, the police went with him up the back stairs and they broke in the back door. She is a schizophrenic and had pushed almost all of her furniture over in a stack against the front door. None of them knew what to do with the poor thing so they took her to the county jail. Obviously, they'll have to do something else today.

OCTOBER 21

Jack's day off and it started off harrowing. We were going to Lexington by way of the Weisenberger Mill Road, when we saw a blue truck that had crashed into a tree about two miles from town. A young man was out walking around with blood all over his face and a girl all bloody and moaning was still in the truck. A police car came roaring up. Jack got out to see if he could help them and the trooper called an ambulance. Just then Eddie Hounchell came tearing up with two bloody tiny children in his car—he had been taking them from the accident to the office when he spotted Jack and me driving out. So, he had turned around and brought them back to be checked out. The children had deep lacerations on the face and head. Jack said they should all go to the hospital. We turned around and followed the ambulance back to town.

NOVEMBER 16

The refrigerator has gone on the blink, and I am dismayed because it means a lot more to me than just an appliance. It is twenty-two years old, and I hate to see it go because it is the only tangible thing I have left of my friend Bob Hicks. In 1961, Matt was running a temperature of one hundred four and craving ice cream. The refrigerator we were using was an old one and wouldn't keep things frozen. So, I called Bob—it was at this time that he, his brother, and Dick Starks were running a business downtown and I told him the size of the space where a new refrigerator would have to fit and asked him to choose one and deliver it for me. I couldn't leave the house as Matt had already had one convulsion with his high fever. Bob delivered this refrigerator and volunteered to sit in the room with Matt while I ran to the grocery to buy the ice cream. There is no other refrigerator that can take its place.

The afternoon that Matt had his convulsion was a terrible time. He had the chicken pox and I heard him making funny little hiccup noises and went to his room to check him. His eyes were rolled back in his head, and he was obviously convulsing.

I grabbed him up and shot to the phone to call Jack to come. He was home in an instant and we were getting Matt into a bathtub of tepid water when Ben came tearing up the steps to see if he could help. The fever broke after a few minutes and Matt was on the way to recovery.

Jack asked me how Jenny was doing as she also had chicken pox and was lying in her bed. I answered, "Oh, she is OK. I just took her temperature, and it was only a hundred and four degrees." Both men pushed by me to check her immediately before heading back to the office.

Exactly one month later Jack was examining an OB patient and she casually asked, "How is your little boy? Did he get over his convulsions OK?"

Jack was surprised that she knew about Matt and said so. She answered, "Oh you were in the middle of examining me that day last month when your nurse came for you with the news about your son. You went running out and Dr. Roach came to finish my exam for you. Then he was told about your boy, and he went tearing out also. Finally, I got tired of waiting and just went on home."

Jack was chagrined but she was nice and said she was just glad to hear that the boy was alright.

DECEMBER 20

Billy and Barbara Grimes had the office staff over for a Christmas Party and spouses were included. They have restored an old house, and it is utterly charming. Her decorations were lovely. We all enjoyed being together as always.

CHRISTMAS DAY

It is eleven o'clock in the morning and I am sitting in the den in the middle of a conglomeration of ribbons, papers, and boxes, along with Jenny, Matt, Peter, Mama, and Tom Bombadil. Ann T is upstairs getting dressed and Jack is at the hospital making rounds before we go to Mom Fisher's. There is a big fire in the fireplace. It was minus eight degrees this morning—an all-time record for Midway on a Christmas morning. The two boys slept on the floor in the den last night and kept the fire going all night. Tom Bombadil slept with them.

1984

Peter will never go out of style.

—Agnes Walcutt

JANUARY 27

Jack was gone all night to the hospital. That doesn't happen often anymore, but I worry when it does.

FEBRUARY 4

Thursday, we took Jim Cogar, Kenney Harper, Jim Thomas, and his friend to the Merrick Inn to celebrate Jim C's seventy-eighth birthday. We were out in the largest room and the noise was distracting to him and to Kenney. But the food was fantastic. The company was even better.

FEBRUARY 12

A friend came home with Ann T from a swim meet and the two of them wanted to fix supper. It consisted of hot dogs, macaroni and cheese, canned cream corn, and Jello chocolate pudding. Need I say more?

FEBRUARY 15

This past January thirty-first one of Jack's favorite old lady patients, Norma Workman, died. She had been a patient of Ben's when we came here twenty-five years ago who could never pay her bill because her husband, Henry, was a tenant farmer who made very little money. She kept herself and her house clean and tried to cope with her life. Jack and Ben continued to see her every time she called even though they never thought much was wrong with her except in her mind. And they were always sympathetic and kind to her. It was easy for me to recognize Norma when she called because she never used the title of "Doctor" when asking for Jack—it was just "Let me talk to Fisher." Or "Is Fisher there?" She was the only one to ever do that and she did it every time.

Another thing I recall about Norma and Henry was when they went anyplace in town, they had to walk, as they did not own a car. I remember how they ambled down the sidewalk— he would walk about five paces ahead of her and they never spoke. To this day when Jack and I are walking, if he gets ahead of me, I will say, "Wait up, Henry," and he knows why I call him that.

FEBRUARY 25

We went to Bruce and Pat's house for supper tonight and I had the time of my life. Bruce was beautiful—just like he used to be, and I've never seen Pat so happy. It was a wonderful evening.

APRIL 3

Pud Haynes called me late last night to tell me that his sister Mary Ann had committed suicide. I don't know what I said to him, but Jack said I was OK. The minute I hung up I cried as hard as I have ever cried in my life, scaring my children, I'm sure.

Mary Ann and I go back to the ninth grade—she was my best friend in school. She was a funny, warm, gentle, and wonderful person, and I can't bear the thought of what she must have gone through while she was planning this. She had closed herself up in the garage and had started the motor of her car. She had left a list in the kitchen of her old friends (me included) that she wanted her brother to call.

I feel an overwhelming loss. And grief. And guilt. I wish I had done more to keep in touch. She has been a steady force, a good friend since 1947—always there in the back of my mind.

MAY 8

Monday, I met Barb Moraja at the Kroger parking lot, and we went to see Chuck Mooney, our surgeon. Delightful fellow. I was A-OK once again. She had a funny looking cyst which he removed and was going to send off for tests. That sort of sent a shadow over our day although Chuck assured her that it looked benign. We had lunch and then went to Mr. Amburgy's and bought our spring flowers. She is to let me know if the cyst is a problem.

MAY 11

Thursday at the crack of dawn Jack went to St. Joseph's in Lexington for Ken Hagan's tests to see if there is blockage around his heart. They had scheduled his test for eight but rescheduled it for ten, so Jack tore back to Woodford Memorial, made rounds, and was back in time for the tests.

Ken's heart shows a great deal of blockage—none from a main artery, so he should have a by-pass. He is the seventh of Jack's good friends to have serious problems with their hearts, and like Ike Rouse says—their single common denominator is that they are all good friends with Jack and probably owe him money. Hmmmm.

MAY 17

We had supper at T.G.I. Friday's and while we were eating back in a corner, we saw a man that was a good friend to Jack's brother, Jim. He was with a sweet young thing who was not his daughter. I was instantly suspicious. When we were finished, we walked around to the window outside where they were sitting without looking at them but making sure they saw us just to make him squirm if he is running around on his lovely wife.

It made me think of Ike Rouse again. One time at a ball game he saw one of his best friends stepping out on his wife, so Ike sidled over to the friend and said to him, "Why hello Perfect Stranger!" Priceless.

MAY 18

Jack had to make a home visit at three-thirty last night on Stella Lacefield, and as he was leaving, she said, "Jack, I guess you and Jo will be the next ones to get a divorce. After all the other's nothing would surprise me now.

"No, Stella," answered Jack. "You and Joe will be next." Considering the fact that Stella and Joe were both well over ninety and he is totally blind and dependent on her, she got a laugh over that one.

MAY 26

Jack saw Billy Frank Baker at the office last week and was called out of the room for a phone call during the exam. When he went back in, Billy Frank was obviously upset. After a few minutes of hedging, he finally admitted that while Jack was out of the room, Billy Frank had sneaked a look at his patient card and his eyes had fallen on the words Jack had written following the previous exam, "Patient is slightly obese."

"Being slightly obese is like being slightly pregnant, Jack," he protested. "Now tell me, am I obese or not?" Jack had a hard time answering tactfully and finally managed to put B.F. on the defensive by telling him that he had no business looking at that card in the first place.

Billy Frank's wife, Jean, is the lady who allows her dog to hop upon the bed beside her when Jack goes to examine her. The great big dog sits there, stock still, growling and baring his teeth at Jack the entire time. Jean smiles and says, "Don't worry, Jack. He never bites." Nevertheless, those exams are the fastest Jack ever makes. Billy Frank and Jean are great people—good friends—and have been since the very first.

JUNE 6

Saw the Walcutt man last night and asked about his mother, who has always been one of my favorite people. She was one of the "Old Guard" of Midway in my salad days and she had been a part of most of the town's activities when she was well. She is now in Florida in a nursing home and is totally senile, so we hear. She will be ninety-two on September fifth. I miss her.

Our book club met at the Busters' last night and I asked Bill to tell us a little about the Normandy Invasion, as he had been involved with it. This week had been the fortieth anniversary. It was fascinating to hear—and I hope I can remember it correctly.

Bill was the head of the "B" Battalion of the Armored Division and did not "go in" until "D-Day Three". They left in their ships from South Hampton around noon on the fifth of June after having to wait for two days because of rains and storms. The channel was really choppy—he was in a British boat. There were literally hundreds of boats that were to converge on the four beaches at Normandy—his was to be the Omaha.

They arrived at their destination around midnight and there was fighting going on all night, causing great trembling and shaking of the ships and the vessel that was next to his went down. The survivors made it to shore.

The boats were all overloaded with men because they were expecting a forty percent loss of the one-hundred-thousand men involved, and they had sent along replacements. There was another Lieutenant Colonel (Bill's rank then) of Bill's rank, to take over in the event Bill was killed. All the tanks, big guns, and bulldozers had been completely waterproofed, and they slid down off the boats into the water. When they reached the beaches, the men were gratified that all the machinery worked.

The hardest thing they encountered was the hedgerows, made up of roots of the trees that were hundreds of years old. These hedgerows encircled squares of about five acres, and the Germans were hidden on the other side. The bulldozers and tanks were helpless against the natural barriers. Finally, a boy from Bill's battalion went back to the beaches and gathered up scrap iron. He welded pieces together like giant scissors and put them on the fronts of the tanks. In this way they were able to cut through the hedgerows and the infantry poured in behind them.

Then Bill said there was a field about three miles by one mile completely filled with Germans. Early one morning hundreds of airplanes came over that field and bombed it. Planes were as far as the eye could see—it was the most awesome thing he had ever witnessed.

He feels that the entire operation might have been threatened except for the fact Hitler had been fooled into thinking we were going in at Calais, and he would not move his armor and men from defending that area. Some of his generals told him that it was a ruse—that the invasion was to happen at Normandy, but he would not listen to them.

War is such an incredible horror. I am convinced that there is no conceivable way to understand it unless you have been there.

JUNE 26

Went to the Archives in Frankfort to research family history until two p.m.—Jack was in Chicago for the day. My jet-setting husband! He was trying to get the hospital back in good standing with the accreditation board. He is so concerned about the hospital now.

AUGUST 10

Jack has been taking care of Peggy Wilds' father during a long bout of illness and last week they lost the battle. Peggy wrote Jack a wonderful letter after her Dad died.

Dear Jack,

You surrounded us with love and tender care for many months. You have no idea how comforting it has been for me to know that any time I needed you, I felt comfortable in calling you, knowing that you would respond to me in a positive manner. When we finally accepted the fact that there was no "cure," we turned to you for "care" that you so warmly bestowed on Dad and us. As Dad said about you several times, "I believe Dr. Fisher really cares about me." That has been so very evident and so felt. We are so grateful to you for loving us. We love you.

AUGUST 29

On Monday I went to the funeral of Agnus Walcutt, aged ninety-two, my old friend from my earliest days in Midway. She and I go all the way back—she was Mrs. Roach's next-door neighbor and best friend. She had a wonderful sense of humor. When I was upset that the artist had painted a period costume on my son Peter instead of his sport coat, Agnes stated, "It is marvelous. Peter will never go out of style." She was right.

One day when we both by chance were visiting Mrs. Roach, who was not feeling well. Mrs. Roach walked into the room and fell flat on the floor in a dead faint. She was a large woman, and Agnes was very small, and I was pregnant with Peter. The two of us tugged and pulled, trying to lift Mrs. Roach up to the couch, but she was solid weight, and we could not budge her. I looked up at Agnes in utter frustration and she was quietly shaking all over with laughter, and I confess, I broke down too. It was just like when two children are in church, and they know it is not the time nor place to get the giggles, but both are totally incapable of anything else. We had a good feeling between us. When I got control of myself, I ran next door to get help for poor Mrs. Roach.

Agnes' funeral was sad. There were not too many of us left who remembered her. The minister read the chapter in Proverbs about the virtuous woman. It was nice but he read from the New Bible—I would have liked the King James version for Agnes.

SEPTEMBER 24

The news is out! Her Royal Highness the Queen of England is going to make a private visit to a horse farm here in Woodford County in October to look at horses and possibly to buy some! We all feel so honored that she is coming here—it is the most exciting news that we have had in a long time.

OCTOBER 9

On Sunday, Queen Elizabeth arrived in Woodford County. Yesterday her motorcade drove through Midway, and everybody was goggled-eyed. Not to be believed. Her Royal Highness in Midway. The owner of the horse farm is a friend to Ben—as well as a patient—and has asked Ben to be the designated doctor during the royal visit. Talk about an honor!

OCTOBER 11

My day to go to the races at Keeneland with Lily May Clark and Hilda Starks, and the Queen is scheduled for a public appearance there. She is to present the cup to the winner of the featured race, and I would give anything to be in a place where I might see her. I adore her enormously and would get a great deal of pleasure out of just looking at her. She has been spotted in Midway all three days she has been in the country, riding in a big black car in a long motorcade, and waving her small, gloved hand at the locals. The talk at the gas station was wonderful:

"I wouldn't walk across the street to see her."

"If it wasn't for the American G.I. there wouldn't be a Queen."

But when Jack asked if they had seen her yet, they both allowed as how they had just "by chance" been over by the railroad tracks the two times she had been going by and yes, they had felt like they ought to wave back at her.

OCTOBER 13

We saw the Queen at the racetrack! Lily May, Hilda and I went early and were standing at a rail after having a hotdog for lunch, and she came walking by all the way down a path with her entourage. I had Matt's camera with the zoom lens and I was having a terrible time getting it focused because she was so much closer than I had predicted when I had Matt to set the thing. Lily May called out, "Bill's binoculars don't work! I can barely see the Queen with them!!" And when we looked over to help her, we saw she had the big end up to her eyes. She looked so funny that we nearly cracked up laughing.

I started clicking the unfocused camera like crazy, just hoping some of the shots would miraculously turn out. Totally unnoticed by us in all the furor, a photographer from the Lexington Herald-Leader snapped a shot of us which appeared in the morning paper—zoom lens, backwards binoculars, and all. We looked like creatures from outer space and can only hope that all the paraphernalia makes us unrecognizable as, thank God, the reporter did not ask our names.

OCTOBER 18

Monday I did chores and cooked all afternoon. I decided to wait up for Jack no matter what, so I ironed until one-fifteen a.m. Several of the doctors in the county are trying to instigate the policy where the factories would sign up with one (or two) doctors and pay them a set salary for their employees' illnesses at a lower cost than the individual doctors pay. Then so much money would come out of every worker's paycheck to cover the expenses of the factory. Jack is horrified. They want him to sign on but he is not interested. He thinks the concept is a giant step towards socialized medicine, and directly opposed to his beloved theme of "fee for service." Jack came home from the meeting as upset as I have ever seen him.

NOVEMBER 25

There always seems to be an elderly female patient who is calling several times a night, time after time, day after day, year after year. Right now, that patient called at four thirty-five a.m. from the hospital just to tell Jack how good she was feeling. We were both just relieved that it wasn't a call for a home visit, and we went back to sleep.

NOVEMBER 28

Jack had an emergency city council meeting Monday— they signed for an $800,000 loan from the government to hook on with the Lexington water works. Ever since our spring ran dry during the summer of 1983 and we had to lay the overland emergency pipes, we have known that something had to be done.

Then it was brought up that a landowner just at the entrance of Midway on US 421 had sent a note asking them to discuss a proposed trucking station that might be established on his property. He had written that it would generate thirty-eight jobs for our town and $160,000 in taxes, as it would have to be annexed to use the sewer lines and water. We are afraid it would change the entire image of the area as it would be an enormous station and it would probably open up Pandora's box out there. But we feel sorry for the landowners as it is believed they genuinely need the money, and this would be a Godsend for them. A quandary.

DECEMBER 3

The hospital had a group from Louisville come up Wednesday to talk about signing on with them, and Jack went to the meeting. The average patient count over there is down from thirty-five to twenty-four daily and there is major concern. Jack is still leery of signing on with a big company. He says you give up so much independence when you do that. He is going to another meeting tonight.

Saturday Jack and I went to a meeting to see what we could do to prevent the trucking company from building an exchange station here. We don't want a big industry right at our front door, but we want to make a totally fair decision. It is a problem.

DECEMBER 26

Last Saturday, I worked all day for the big family dinner to be held here on Sunday. Saturday night we went to church but had to skip a party afterwards as Jack had two OBs to go in at the last minute. Sunday morning, he delivered both babies from five until ten-thirty a.m. and was on hand to greet the Louisville crew when they arrived. They seemed to enjoy the meal and we played Trivial Pursuit all afternoon.

For Christmas this year, Jack gave me a black sweater and I gave him an all-weather jogging suit. When we came back from Louisville yesterday, we ran out to see Jim Cogar for a minute. He was alone and had waited for us to come to open his packages, so we were doubly glad we had gone.

Ahead of the Hounds

1985

It was a turnaround for me to see that medicine could indeed be practiced as a loving art.

—Becca Lewis, Office Student

JANUARY 1

Yesterday a patient of Ben's sent a check for twenty-five hundred dollars to the office as a gift because they are always willing to treat indigent people. Ben is trying to decide how to divide it up between the doctors and the staff.

JANUARY 15

Went to the city council meeting last night having to do with the trucking station and more than fifty-five people crowded into that small room to protest its coming. As the meeting started, the mayor announced that there would be no trucking station there at Midway. That the man in charge had called to say that he had gotten wind of all the protests, and they would not come where they were not wanted. We couldn't believe our ears. We had won the battle without firing a shot.

I sat in front of the fire talking with Jack a long time last night after the meeting. Medicine is taking such a socialistic turn with the formation of all these "groups" and "plans." Jack does not want any part of the change, but he does not want to lose his good old patients by not being available on the Texas Instruments list, or I.B.M., or whatever. It really is a problem.

JANUARY 22

Monday, I rode to Versailles with Jack and went to the grocery there while he was at the hospital because the roads were so bad. When I came home, Ann Lewis called needing help at the office as the phone was ringing off the wall. Dr. Jim had had an accident out by where Versailles Road meets Midway's. He wanted his Dad to come to the hospital to sew up his head and Ann was the only girl at the office because the other girls couldn't handle the Midway Road.

I am meeting Jack and Becca Lewis for lunch—she is to be the senior student taking her rotation of family practice here at the clinic for the next month.

JANUARY 23

Ate lunch with Jack and Becca yesterday and really enjoyed it. She is having a ball at the office—loves the whole town, as I knew she would.

Jack pierced Ann T's ears last night and she let out 'piercing' screams.

FEBRUARY 5

Jack went to a meeting last night where two doctors were trying to get everyone to sign up to be physicians for the plants and factories for a guaranteed salary. Jack, so far, still wants no part of it.

FEBRUARY 13

Ben came in the office yesterday telling Jack that he has decided to sign up with the Lexington group in their "plan." I feel sorry for Jack as this is not what he wants to do, and he isn't sure that Ben can belong without the other two partners because of the way their practice is set up. Jack isn't sure who is right—there are arguments for both sides.

MARCH 1

Becca's rotation is over, and she sent Jack a beautiful letter. Her last paragraph:

> *Jack, I hope you know what a special physician I think you are. I think I had become jaded and bitter through medical school and work in a large, impersonal medical center. You embody all the ideals I dreamed about when I decided to go to med school and had decided were unrealistic. It was a turnaround for me to see that medicine could indeed be practiced as a loving art.*

Becca is a very special person and much more than just another student to Jack and me.

APRIL 15

Jack went to his high school reunion in Louisville but had to come home early as he had an OB go in. She finally delivered at eleven p.m., and he came home exhausted to eat a cold supper at eleven-thirty, fixed by yours truly. We were still sitting at the table when Jim Cogar called saying he was "feeling funny." So, Jack went out there to check on him. At twelve-thirty, Stella Lacefield called, and Jack went down to make a home visit. She called back at two o'clock and then at three, asking both times if she could "take another pill."

After the three o'clock call, I unplugged Jack's phone and came down to the den couch to be ready to answer the next call. It came not too long after I moved down, and it was Stella asking if it was time to take another pill. I was really nice to her—she is ninety-two, scared and lonely, but the next day would be Monday and Jack simply had to have some rest. He wasn't even on call. I told her she must not call again—she would have to find some other way to determine when her pills were due. That Jack would not be available to her the rest of the night. She then asked me what time it was, and I honestly replied that I did not want to know.

MAY 15

Went with Jack to Louisville for him to attend medical meetings. The final lecture was given by Dr. William DeVries, the doctor who had been doing the artificial heart operations. He is the most charming, intriguing man. He is a true believer in what he is doing. He seems driven to accomplish the thing he said Charles Lindberg spent the last fourteen years of his life trying to develop. It is fascinating—and I got to hold an artificial heart. I was totally won over.

MAY 16

While walking our dog, Tom Bombadil, at Jim Cogar's farm, he ran way ahead of me in the top field—then he stopped dead still and grew rigid with his tail pointed up and stiff, but he was not barking. He was staring across the fence where there was standing a beautiful red fox. They were just staring at one another, almost not daring to breathe. The fox was the same color as Tom, but half as large with a lovely, pointed face and a huge red tail. I was about thirty feet from them. I felt as though you could have heard a pin drop the air was so still. I would have given anything for a camera—the fox was simply magnificent. When I finally called to Tom he came right away, glad to get out of a confrontation.

MAY 23

Jack came in saying that Joe Lehman had had a coronary, and he sent him on up to St. Joseph's. Joe is seventy-six—I would never have guessed it. His vital signs were normal, but he had had pain all night and would not bother Jack until daylight. His EKG was very erratic.

MAY 28

Went to visit Joe Lehman with Jack and he looks wonderful. He is anxious to get home.

JUNE 10

We went to the annual hospital picnic up at Ben's farm yesterday. While we were there, three Greyhound buses wrecked on Pisgah Pike and thirty-six people were injured.

Every available doctor at the picnic had to make a beeline for the hospital.

JUNE 10

Went to Miss Honeywood Rouse's eighty-seventh birthday party, and it was lovely. She sat in a chair in the great hall and "received" like royalty, which she most certainly is. Her granddaughter Amy had prepared all the food, and it was good. All the old guard of Midway appeared.

JULY 3

Today, Jack had his first patient to say that he had gone with a health plan and could he please have his file. Jack reluctantly handed it over. Hope the change doesn't come too fast, but it is definitely in the wind. The man kept apologizing.

JULY 9

Jack had an OB today who is very toxic and having a really hard time. He talked to an obstetrician in consultation, and that doctor said to send her on up to the university hospital. That there was a good chance the mother might die, or the baby, or both, and she should be where the best equipment is available. He said that Jack was setting himself up for a lawsuit if he didn't send her.

Jack went to talk to the patient and her husband, and they won't go. They are missionaries from Honduras, and they have no insurance, can barely pay the fee at the office, much less the university's. They said they have a lot of faith in God and in Jack, and they want to stay. The obstetrician told Jack not to call him in to help if there is trouble. So that is how Jack's July ninth is stacking up.

JULY 10

The OB family finally agreed to go to Lexington and the baby girl was delivered by Cesarian—both the mother and the baby are doing fine. Jack went up and sat with the husband, as he was too late to scrub in.

AUGUST 4

My second present from Jack for my birthday was a blue sweatshirt with the logo "Dust Don't Interest Me" written on the front. I think he is trying to tell me something!

AUGUST 21

We had a big celebration tonight. It was a farewell dinner as Matt is on his way to practice dentistry in Fort Lauderdale, and we are leaving today to take Ann T to college at Texas Christian University in Fort Worth. Around five p.m. Jack had to leave to deliver a baby, but there was no problem with the delivery, and he was home to cook steaks by six-thirty.

However, he was called to deliver another baby, whose father he had delivered years ago, and Matt and Jenny took over the grilling. Jack missed the big final dinner. The rest of us sat around looking at old photograph albums laughing, and Jack came in at nine-thirty.

SEPTEMBER 8

I asked Jack last night who was his most unforgettable patient, and he answered without batting an eye naming a woman patient. Asked to elaborate he went on.

He told me that one day she came in the office saying blood was in her urine and she wanted to go to the hospital. It tested out that this was true, and Jack admitted her only to find out in the hospital that there was no kidney stone and also no more blood. They came to the conclusion that she was pricking her finger in the restroom at the office and dropping a little blood into the receptacle because she absolutely loved lying up in bed in the hospital getting all the attention.

He said that another time he was called to see her when she lived with her mother, and she had a big bucket by the couch where she declared she had been vomiting blood. He checked her thoroughly and couldn't find anything wrong, but when he looked in the bucket, there was a large amount of "coffee grounds vomitus" the hallmark of a bleeding ulcer. He sent her immediately to the hospital where she stayed several days with nothing showing up on all the tests, so Jack supposed that she had put actual coffee grounds in the bucket before he came to see her.

Later on, she went to another doctor who was also on staff at Woodford Memorial (after Jack was on to all her tricks) and she was admitted one day as his patient. She stayed until her Medicaid ran out and the committee asked that she be made to leave, but she requested a hearing where she might plead her case.

Jack happened to be on that committee at the time, and he vows that she came walking feebly into the room with an emesis basin in one hand and a rosary in the other, looking as if she were in great pain. The one doctor who did not know her looked aghast but the other two knew her well and were totally unimpressed—except by her ingenuity.

It was she and her kind that drove Alex Alexander to distraction when he was practicing at the office, and he was utterly flabbergasted the first day he went to the university hospital to work when she appeared on his elevator and smiled a weak and knowing smile at him. Jack hasn't heard a word from her in years and he is not complaining.

DECEMBER 7

Last night we went to a large dinner party—there were twenty-six people there and it was lovely. Just as Jack and I started to sit down to eat, Mr. E.V. Benjamin slid from his chair to the floor, and Dr. Crutcher knelt over him. Jack ran to help and the two doctors frantically worked several minutes—it seemed endless—to get him breathing again. He was choking on a piece of meat and when he passed out, he clamped his teeth together. Jack and Dick couldn't get their finger in his mouth and couldn't get him to respond to the Heimlich Maneuver. He turned blue in the face. Guests were all staring, ashen, thinking he was dying—sure that he was gone. Jack finally rammed his fist in E.V.s mouth and brought out a large piece of beef and the color flushed back in his face, although he still remained unconscious. E.V. is an elderly man and not in basic good health to begin with.

An ambulance was called and Jack rode with him to the hospital missing out on the great dinner. After a very subdued meal, I drove the car over to the hospital to collect Jack, breaking a lifelong promise not to drive a car after having had even just one drink.

DECEMBER 16

Wednesday night we met Ben and Toss at their house on the farm and Ben said that Jack is the standard against which Toss measures all other men. What a responsibility.

DECEMBER 27

Friday night we went to an open house at Nancy Jefferson's, one of the lovely ladies who works at the office. Her house was all decorated and the food was divine. Ben's patient-friend in Lexington had given the office staff another twenty-five hundred dollars for taking care of indigent people, and Ben had divided it among the girls as well as with the doctors. Nancy had taken her portion and had given a party for all of us to enjoy. What a fitting way for us to end our social calendar for 1985.

1986

I cannot imagine Midway without the Lehman family.
> —Ben Chandler in The Woodford Sun

JANUARY 11

My old buddy Jeanette Lehman is in the hospital about to die. Her blood pressure has dropped to sixty, she has a tracheostomy to help her to breathe, her kidneys have failed, and she is full of tubes and needles. Last Saturday she was at the shop when she started to choke. One of the girls who work there called Jack and he went right away. He sent her immediately to St. Joseph's Hospital in Lexington and she has been under the care of her heart specialist ever since. She now seems to be failing altogether. It breaks my heart.

JANUARY 28

Miss Jeanette died on Monday around one a.m. My good friend. She and Mr. Tom Roach were my first friends in Midway and I will truly miss her. Many days when I didn't have anything to do, I'd walk down to the shop and visit with Miss Jeanette. She was always glad to see me—would stop anything she was doing to sit down and chat with me. She worked Saturday morning before entering the ICU on Wednesday and died less than three weeks later. A most remarkable lady.

JANUARY 31

Watched TV last night and quilted while I waited for Jack to come in. He was called back out at two a.m. to see Joe Lehman, who was in heart failure. Jack stayed with him for an hour—Joe was scared to death. He had built up fluid but had a kidney infection and couldn't "go." So, he couldn't take a fluid pill. Jack went to the office to get the oxygen unit. I'm sure he misses Miss Jeanette because they had always lived in the big old house together, as neither had ever married. He is to see his heart specialist today—he looked ghastly at Miss Jeanette's funeral on Wednesday.

FEBRUARY 1

Today I am beginning to read all my old journals in preparation of writing on my book in earnest. The time has come to either do it or to stop talking and thinking about it.

FEBRUARY 4

Jack is sick again. He coughs constantly and sounds completely stopped up. We have cancelled out on going to Jim Cogar's as he was afraid he might give his "bug" to Jim. Last night he came home from the office late, ate and went straight to bed. He was called at eleven because one of his OBs had come in bleeding even though she wasn't due until February thirteenth. She had lost about three pints of blood, so he called an OB man and they decided to do a section. Jack was so worried because the baby's heartbeat was slower than the mother's. She was thirty-three and this was her first baby—sometimes a cause for concern. So, he called in a pediatrician because he thought resuscitation would probably be necessary and he did not want to do it because he felt so sick.

It turned out that it was her liver that was bleeding, so he had to call in a surgeon! Both mother and baby survived, none the worse for wear. Jack came in at four-thirty and I persuaded him to skip his seven-thirty staff meeting and sleep in until eight.

FEBRUARY 26

Joe Lehman leaned back in his chair at the shop this morning and died—less than one month after the death of his sister, Miss Jeanette. We guess it was the result of a heart attack—he was dead before anyone got to him. His death brings an end to the Lehman name in Midway, a family that had been there one hundred and thirty-two years. The ancestor who first located here came to Midway in 1854 and was a builder, as well as owner of a furniture shop and a mortuary. He built many houses and churches here and his son carried on the businesses when his father died. The old man was the grandfather of Elizabeth, Jeanette, Joe, and William.

MARCH 7

Ben Chandler wrote in his newspaper column in the Woodford Sun this week about the Lehman family:

Miss Elizabeth, Miss Jeanette, and Joe were the ones we all saw at their unique store in Midway in recent years. The Lehman's Store during my lifetime has been the most unusual and was the single most important reason for attracting people to the village of Midway for many, many years. Items for sale came from all over the world as the owners traveled many times to Europe and elsewhere on buying trips. Quality was assured at Lehman's and its fine reputation spread far and near by word of mouth.

I cannot imagine Midway without the Lehman family. I cannot imagine going into that store and not seeing Miss Jeanette or Joe, it took years to get used to not seeing Miss Elizabeth.

It is incredibly sad to see the name end in this community. Their niece from Atlanta will take over the shop and its operation. She has three sons, so we hope the shop in all its excellence will continue—but of course, their name is not Lehman, so the name is gone from Midway. They meant so much to many people—they will be sorely missed.

MARCH 28

Last night Jack and I were walking Tom Bombadil after supper, and we were down by Mrs. Ford's house. Suddenly a long, shiny black car screeched to a halt and two big men jumped out at us. It really gave me a start. Then they both began talking at once, very excited, and we finally found out what was wrong.

"It's the preacher, Dr. Fisher!"

"He has fallen out!"

Jack told them that he would have to get his bag, so I took Tom's leash and Jack literally ran home along with one of the men. The man had on a suit and tie and hard-soled shoes—I could not imagine how hard it was on his feet to run that fast.

MARCH 29

At six-thirty this morning the phone rang, and a lady asked Jack to come to Winter Street right away as Stella Lacefield was dying. Jack put on his clothes and quickly left. As his car was rounding the corner, the phone rang again, and a lady's voice asked if he had left the house yet. I said he had, and she groaned and hung up.

When Jack arrived at the Lacefield house, Stella was sitting up in bed laughing and talking and very much revived. The lady who was staying with her had been doing all the phoning, and she was chagrined and offered Jack a cup of coffee.

This episode reminded us of the morning several years ago when the phone rang early in the morning, and a man quietly asked Jack to come—that his mother there in the Ford house down our street had just passed away. Jack quickly went out. Just as Jack backed out of the driveway, the phone rang again. I answered it, and a man's voice anxiously asked to speak to the doctor.

"He isn't here." I answered. "He is down the street where an elderly lady has just passed away."

"Oh, God," the man moaned and slowly hung up the phone. In a minute Jack was home. When he had gone in the Ford place, the lady was sitting up in her bed, smiling and talking, while her son stood around shaking his head, grinning and being very embarrassed. She lived quite a while after that.

MAY 21

The Queen of England, Her Royal Highness, Elizabeth is due to arrive here in Woodford County to make her second visit to the horse farm belonging to Ben's good friend, Will Farish. She is to spend four or five days here on business and pleasure, and the entire county is really spiffing up. The Episcopal church in Versailles where she will attend the services on Sunday, is in a total uproar.

The church has been hurriedly putting down new walks, new flowers and shrubs and painting everything in sight. The parishioners have been sent invitations which they must present at the door on Sunday to get in, and they must be recognized by a designated church person at the door to be who the invitation says they are, and no one under twelve years old will be admitted. Everyone must be seated in their pew before the Queen starts to enter and no one may leave until she leaves.

The security people are thoroughly examining the church of course, and the Baptist church which sets very close by, has also been scrutinized.

The entire place is in a happy, excited state of commotion—the Queen will be visiting three or four horse farms here in the county, and we all think it is pretty wonderful. In my humble opinion, she is the finest example of "class" left in the world today, and the rest of us can only stand by and admire her. She has made very few mistakes.

In light of this, the White House called the office yesterday! Ben's name had been sent in as the official doctor for the Queen and her entourage—as it was for the previous visit—and the White House wanted to make sure Ben was prepared. Barbara Grimes allowed as how he was. It is all such great fun. The ultimate way to begin a summer.

MAY 27

Saturday night we were driving towards the Old Frankfort Pike and there was a state police traffic block just the other side of Jim Cogar's. It was for the Queen and her motorcade (seven black Lincoln Continentals), and we watched with awe from a distance as they turned into Smiser and Kashie West's farm. Isn't that fantastic!

Sunday, we went to Louisville to Jack's sister's house for a dinner she was having for all the cousins. Ben was on call for the Queen and Jim was for the practice, so Jack felt secure about leaving. About seven-thirty the phone rang, and it was Ann T simply frantic. One of the Queen's attendants was sick, and they could not locate Ben or Jim. Ann T told them to sit tight, and she would find her dad, all the time thinking that this was one of her friends playing a trick on her.

Jack called the number back—it was the Marriott Hotel where some of the Queen's group were staying—and it was not a prank. The Queen's footman (what in the world does a footman do these days and times?) was seriously ill and the problem was that they had been given a wrong number to call the hospital for Ben. Jack called the hospital for them and told the desk operator to page Ben on both beepers and if they couldn't reach him in five minutes to call back—that it was urgent.

They called in an instant saying they had located Ben, and he was on his way to the Marriott. Jack called the English people back to report this, but they informed him that the man was hurting so bad that they had sent him in an ambulance to Woodford Memorial! So, Jack called the hospital once again and told them to intercept Ben on the beeper and have him come to the hospital instead. What a comedy of errors. We figured Jack owed his sister at least twenty-five dollars for the phone bill.

The uproar simply made our party. Every time the phone rang later that night, one of the cousins would say, "Grab that quick. It's probably Elizabeth calling back." It was great fun.

MAY 31

It is now one o'clock in the morning, and I am too upset to sleep. I thought I'd write in my journal before I go to bed.

We went to the restaurant downtown tonight with "B" and Pat Williams and we were sitting around enjoying ourselves after dinner when Ben Roach came in searching for Jack and me—looking like the 'wrath of God'. He had been in the hospital in Lexington to have a routine prostate operation and we had not heard the results of the tests. Jack and I went out in the hall with him, and the news was grim.

The tests showed a large, inoperable cancer in the urethra, which they said could not be treated with chemotherapy or radiation. They said they will run more tests to see if there is spread. If there is, they can do nothing. If there is no spread, they will do very radical surgery and hope for the best. He said with no spread there is a twenty percent chance of survival for five years. Ben is almost sixty-eight years old, but he has never aged to any of us—and we thought he would be around for at least twenty more years. Last month he was optimistically planting small trees up at the farm for heaven's sake.

He broke down a couple of times while he was talking to us. He explained to me that cancers are graded on a scale of one to four, with the four being the most severe, and his was measured a three. He said that he had called all his children, and they were on the way.

Then Ben left to go back to the hospital, and we managed to get through the rest of the evening somehow. It was wonderful being with such good friends as "B" and Pat. When they went home, Jack and I walked around Midway until midnight with Tom Bombadil in an utter state of shock. The lights were on up at Jim's house, so Jack knocked on the door. Jim's wife, Dee Dee answered the door, saying "Come on in. There'll be no sleeping in this house tonight."

When something like this happens, all the good times come flooding back over you. When we first came here the Roaches made up so much of our lives—we played cards with them every Sunday night and went out with them at least one more night every week. Ben has a wonderful sense of humor about the practice and about himself, acting with a marvelous sensitivity about human frailty. He has become as dear to us as family and my heart is breaking as this is happening to him.

When I went to the office to answer the phones for them two weeks ago, I walked into the middle room and there sat Jack and Ben at the table going over their patients' charts out loud together just like they did twenty-seven years ago. Then Ben went out into the waiting room, smiling and patting everyone on the back, calling them all by name. That is a custom he has always taken time for no matter how busy he is and the patients love it.

Ben has always been so very caring for his patients. So gentle and kind, and quick to the rescue when needed. One of his beliefs is that even if you cannot always cure a patient, you can, always comfort him—and Ben has practiced this creed religiously. The other thing about him is that he has always been so very lucky. Things just seem to fall right for him every time no matter what. I can't believe that his luck has finally run out on him now. We are praying for a miracle.

JUNE 3

Am mentally exhausted. Utterly. Ben is going back into the hospital for tests for spread. He is going to Sloane-Kettering in New York for a second opinion on Thursday because of the rarity of this type of cancer. He is doing something anyway and seems in control and in good spirits.

Tonight, Jack was trying to cheer me up and he told me two funny stories that happened to him this week. One was about Sue Dunavent who called practically hysterical. She gasped out, "Dr. Fisher! Come over immediately! When I got up this morning my heart was racing. Now it is not beating at all—Hurry!!!"

Then a patient of his that is one hundred and three years old and is living at Taylor Manor. She was looking closely at him as he bent down to examine her, and she exclaimed, "Dr. Fisher! Your hair is all gone!!" These stories helped but nothing could really lift our spirits tonight. Too much on our minds.

JUNE 14

A letter has arrived at the office and the return address is "Buckingham Palace." It read:

9th June 1986
Dear Dr. Roach,

Paul Burnell has now returned safely to London, and the Queen has commanded me to send you her warm thanks for all your help to him. Her Majesty was very sad to hear that you yourself had been struck down, and sends you her warmest good wishes for your recovery.

It was signed *Yours Sincerely, Kenneth*—the second name was not quite clear. We were all totally impressed.

JUNE 24

Jack came home last night as crestfallen as I have ever seen him, simply bowled over. Jim told him that his malpractice insurance is going up in July—would increase from three thousand dollars a year to more than eleven thousand—due to obstetrics primarily. As Jim delivers about ten OB's a year, he could not justify that expense, and no one can argue that. But it means that Jack will also have to give it up because of the way the practice is set up. As no other family doctor in the county has been able to continue obstetrics, he would not be able to find anyone to cover for him. This has knocked him for a row of bricks. This is the end of an era for him—OBs have been the joy of his practice from the very beginning.

The insurance craze is spiraling up at great bounds and it is changing the medical fabric of our society. Doctors are beginning to have to practice on the defensive in all areas and the cost of doing this is astronomical. The patient is the loser much more than the doctor. I worry about the young pregnant girls who are just starting out in their lives and having the burden of the expense of an obstetrician, which is more than double the cost at the office. The pendulum is bound to swing back, but probably too late to benefit Jack. Our office was one of the last in Kentucky where family practitioners delivered babies. Something has got to give. Someone has to stand up and say "enough".

JULY 4

Jack and I were walking tonight down by the Baptist church, and a young, maybe sixteen-year-old boy came up to us obviously scared, and said he was lost. He had no idea where he was. Jack recognized him as being a child he had delivered years ago—the parents had named him Norman in honor of Jack—and he goes to a special school in Louisville because he is legally blind. He was trying to find a friend's house in Midway, had gotten lost, and was panicked. We offered to call his mother to come for him, but he said she did not have a car. He was absolutely frantic. So, he walked home with us, and "Good old Jack" got in our car and drove him home.

PART FOUR

Epilogue

Ahead of the Hounds

256

Don't look back. Something might be gaining on you.
—Satchel Paige

There is no mistake about it, Satchel Paige was right when he said, "Don't look back. Something might be gaining on you." And to my way of thinking, one of the things he could have been thinking about is the "hound" of unwanted change in our lives that keeps nipping at our heels causing us to run faster and faster in a direction that is not always what we would have otherwise chosen.

Clearly the field of medicine is one area in our lives where change is rampant, whether we like it or not. Along with all the wonderful discoveries and advances in technology and new cures, rules and regulations have come that strangle and limit both the doctor and the patient in ways totally unheard of twenty-five years ago. Jack has lost many battles with change in his beloved family practice. He can no longer deliver babies due to the astronomical rise in insurance premiums, he was unable to stay independent of all health groups and to keep his personal standard of "fee for service rendered." HMO's, PPOs, increased malpractice insurance premiums, Medicare, Medicaid, and the like and so on, are all intervening between him and his patient, making decisions for both of them which could and should be made by the doctor and the person under his care.

So far, however, Jack has been able to work within the boundaries of these changes without altering the time spent with his patient. The basic foundation of Jack's practice is that when he closes the door of an examining room and prepares to care for the sick, it is just the two of them working together, combating the pain and misery of disease. That person, whether suffering from the common cold or lung cancer, has Jack's total attention as long as they are talking together in that room. All the changes in medicine that have been, or will be, can never alter that basic approach to medicine that Jack has taken to be his own. He has dedicated his life to this standard.

The most devastating thing that has ever happened to Jack in the world of his practice came this spring when he learned that Ben had transitional-cell prostatic cancer, which is possibly incurable. Ben has always been such a vital part of our lives—virtually becoming a loving part of our family—that it is impossible to think of Midway or the practice without him. He is optimistic about his illness, trying a new combination of four chemotherapeutic agents, and we have every reason to believe that this will reverse the dreadful first prognosis. He is feeling well enough at this time to come to the office for a few hours in the mornings, putting on his white coat and doing the thing that he has loved and done so well for thirty-nine years.

In the field of personal relationships, we have dealt with disease and disappointments. We have sorrowed over the passing of old friends who were so much a part of our lives and of the life of Midway but who are now gone. They have taken with them some of the distinctive quality that was once our town and can never be replaced. But we have a healthy respect for the new generation coming on, and they appear to be emerging as kind and caring human beings, with decent priorities, and a willingness to stand up for the things in which they believe.

The "hound" of unwanted change is always howling at our door in the area of our beautiful town and county. We have lost the struggle to keep the big trucks from racing through our main street more frequently than they used to due to an Interstate highway coming within a mile of our boundary. Townhouses on the edge of Midway have forever altered the character of that entrance into town. Right now, because of a huge automobile factory coming to a neighboring county, we are being threatened with the widening of our lovely Midway-Versailles Road, or with the continuation of the Pisgah Pike through farms that have been designated historically significant land. Neither choice is acceptable, and we are drawing our swords once again.

In spite of these disappointments, we have managed to stand together and to hold on to the things we deem most dear about our surroundings. We have been able to stay a community with "old-time" caring for our neighbors, and of keeping priorities on human relationships, even in the face of an ever-changing world.

In trying to sum up all of this, I am reminded of the story that Senator Everett Dirkson of Illinois told in 1968 when he was running for re-election. He appeared to be losing when the early returns were coming in and a reporter asked him how he felt about his chances. The Senator replied that he was like the Irishman, who, when falling from the top of a fourteen-story building, heard his friend calling out of a window on the tenth floor as he went sailing by, "So far, Mike, you're alright!"

With this story in mind, Jack and I can look back at our relentlessly pursuing "hounds" and say, "So far, we are alright." So far.

ABOUT THE AUTHOR

JONELLE JONES FISHER (Jo) was born in Lyon County, Kentucky, in the summer of 1933. She moved with her family to Louisville when she was twelve years old, and graduated from the University of Louisville in 1954. She and Norman S. (Jack) Fisher married in 1956 just after his sophomore year in medical school. When his training was completed in 1959, they moved with their two children to Midway, Kentucky where he began his practice.